Edexcel AS History Un.. .

Republicanism, Civil War and Francoism in Spain, 1931–75

Robin Bunce, Peter Callaghan and Laura Gallagher

Series editors: Derrick Murphy and Angela Leonard

STUDENT BOOK

A PEARSON COMPANY

Contents

Introduction

Welcome to History at AS level. History is a fascinating subject, concerned with the world as it was and how it became the world we know now. By studying history, you will encounter new people, new places, new societies and cultures – even though they are all in the past. If you have an enquiring mind and an interest in the world around you then History is the subject for you.

How to make the most of the course

- Practise your skills. History is not just about learning information or about telling the story of what happened in the past. You need to be able to understand and explain why things turned out the way they did and about how much they changed. The Skills Builder sections in this book will help you do this.
- Prepare for debate and discussion. Historians do not always agree about why events or developments in the past happened, or about their importance – so don't be afraid to debate with your teacher and other students. But remember that you must give evidence to support any point you make.
- Use the course book. This book has been designed to help you build up the skills, knowledge and understanding to help you do well in your exam – so use it. See the 'How this book will help you' section overleaf for details.
- Read around the subject. The more you learn about a period of history, the more interesting it becomes. Further reading on your chosen topics will broaden your understanding of the period, give you better insights into causation and change, and make the course much more rewarding.

What you will learn

Unit 1 focuses on historical themes in breadth. This means that you need to be able to understand and explain why things changed over a fairly long period. In Option E4/F4 you will focus on the Spanish Civil War and the way in which it affected the development of modern Spain. First, you will consider the causes of the civil war, the long-term causes rooted in the nature of Spain's society, politics and economics, and the more immediate causes which emerged during the Second Republic. Second, you will consider the immediate triggers of the civil war in the early part of 1936 and the relative strength, in terms of resources and popular support, of the opposing sides at the outbreak of the civil war. Third, you will examine the nature of the civil war and the reasons why the Nationalists won. Specifically, you will study the outlines of the major battles, the role of Franco, leader of the Nationalists, the significance of political divisions on the Republican side and the role played by foreign powers during the war. Finally, you will study Franco's rule, from his victory in the civil war in 1939 to his death in 1975. This includes considering the impact of the war years on Spain, the New State's use of repression and terror, and the changing role of groups such as the Falange and the Church in Spanish society.

You will also consider the effectiveness of the government's economic policy, the transition from dictatorship to monarchy and the role of Juan Carlos up until Franco's death in 1975.

How you will be assessed

For Unit 1 you will take a written exam. You will write two essays: one on each topic you have studied (i.e. one on Spain 1931–75 and one on your other chosen topic). For each topic you will have a choice of two questions. You will have 1 hour and 20 minutes in total, or 40 minutes for each essay.

How this book will help you

- Clearly written text gives you the historical information you need for this topic in the right amount of depth.
- 'Take note' boxes indicate when you should make notes of your own. These notes will help you with the activities and can also form the basis of your revision, so it's worth keeping up to date with these as you go along.
- Activities help you understand the content and build up your historical skills.
- Skills Builder sections help you develop the essential skills you need to do well in your exam.
- Examzone tells you what you need to know to prepare for the exam, including:
  - what to expect on the day
  - how to revise
  - what the assessment objectives mean and how you can meet them
  - what the different levels mean and how you can gain a high mark
  - example essays with examiner commentaries to help you understand what the examiners are looking for and how to use your information.

Map showing regions of Spain

Chapter 1: **Spain in 1931**

Key questions

- How accurate is it to describe Spain in 1931 as a bitterly divided country?
- What reasons were there for popular discontent in Spain in 1931?
- To what extent was Spain in 1931 'backward'?

Between 1936 and 1939, Spain experienced a bloody and violent civil war, inflicting terrible scars on the country which are still felt today. In a BBC documentary in 2009, British politician Michael Portillo, whose father had fled Spain during the war, commented that, for most of us, Spain is a place we visit to forget the troubles of the world. However, throughout Spain tens of thousands of bodies lie in unmarked mass graves, victims of a bloody civil war and a brutal dictatorship.

In 1931 the Spanish monarchy came to an end and the Second Republic was proclaimed – with much popular support and optimism. But by 1936 the hopes of the Republicans were swallowed up by their opponents and a military coup developed into violent civil war. The rebels were determined to turn back the clock and undo the work of the Republic. How did the war come about? What problems faced the Second Republic in the years 1931–36 and what led to the failure of their government?

To understand the history of the civil war, it is important to grasp the problems that faced Spain and her people in 1931.

Take note

As you read through this chapter, make brief notes on each of the issues raised. When you have completed your notes, create a spider diagram of the problems which faced Spain in 1931.

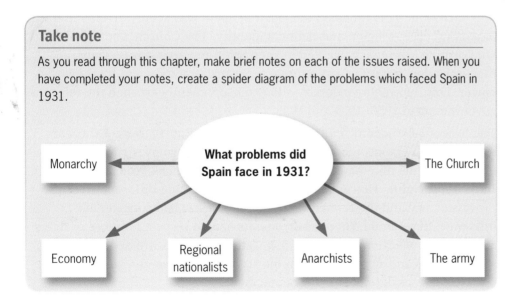

The economy

Compared with the rest of Western Europe in 1931, Spain's economy was backward, fairly primitive and undeveloped. Over half the population lived off the land, often in desperate poverty. Life was a constant struggle simply to survive. In the south of Spain, notably in Andalusia, farming was carried out on vast estates known as *latifundia*.

Ownership of land

In the nineteenth century, the Catholic Church had been deprived of its land, and most of the aristocratic class sold their large estates to the wealthy middle classes.

Glossary

Great Depression

A major economic depression, originating in America in 1929 and lasting until the early 1940s.

Individual rights

A political doctrine which asserts there are certain freedoms and privileges which belong to every individual and should be respected.

These were usually **owned** by rich merchants and businessmen, who were concerned only to make a profit from their investment. They employed landless labourers on a daily basis, most of whom were employed only during the seasons of sowing and harvesting; for the rest of the year their life was a constant struggle to fend off hunger and starvation.

There was, however, some industrial development in the north and north-east of the country. There was a thriving coal mining industry in the northern province of Asturias, and textiles and foreign trade both flourished in Catalonia. However, widespread poverty throughout Spain meant that there was little demand for consumer goods and this prevented the development of a modern industrial economy. Working and living conditions in towns and cities were poor. Wages were low, and there was no social care provided for the unemployed or sick. Basic amenities such as sanitation, street lighting and schools barely existed in most cities.

The new Republic was in serious economic difficulties from the outset. The previous government had spent lavishly on impressive public works schemes in the late 1920s, and left a large budget deficit to its successors. Moreover, the **Great Depression**, which began in the USA in 1929, had spread throughout Europe by the early 1930s. Spain was hit hard. Spanish exports and its industrial production both fell dramatically during the life of the Republic, and unemployment grew rapidly. The new government therefore had a mountain to climb in 1931 to restore prosperity to a fractious Spain.

The political culture of Spain before 1931

Spain was no stranger to civil war. Between 1830 and 1939, Spain experienced four such wars. This reflected the fact that Spain was deeply divided in terms of politics, class, religion and national identity. The Church, and the old land-owning aristocracy, wanted to keep Spain much as it was. They saw modernisation and reform as a threat to Spanish tradition and their own power. This informal reactionary alliance had violently crushed the reformist governments of 1856, 1874 and 1923.

The lack of a democratic culture in Spain was another reason for the war. In Britain and France, there had been a widening popular participation in politics in the nineteenth century and an acceptance of the doctrine of **individual rights**. However, Spanish politics was quite different. In Spain, the aristocracy and the Roman Catholic Church still had considerable influence. In general terms, the aristocrats had no respect for ideas of rights and equality. Additionally, the Roman Catholic Church stressed community, shared values and submission to authority. In this sense, the values of these powerful groups did not support democracy.

The middle class, who tended to support democracy in Britain and France, were weaker in Spain and sometimes opposed democracy. Following the 1850s, there was widespread intermarriage between the new middle class and the old aristocracy. This alliance was further strengthened following 1917, when both groups came together in opposition to working class strikes and peasant risings.

Thus, in 1923, they supported the dictatorship of Primo de Rivera (see page 10). In the 1930s, both groups looked back to the dictatorship as a golden age of order and economic growth, and many believed that the army coup of 1936 would return Spain to these disciplined and prosperous times.

The ruling elites

The monarchy

Spain became a **constitutional monarchy** in 1837. However, from the very beginning, some Spanish monarchs found it difficult to accept this. Queen Isabella, who ascended the throne aged three in 1833, interfered in both domestic and foreign policy in an underhand way, playing off one minister against another. Her disregard for constitutional government, coupled with her notorious private life, led to a rising against her in 1868. Isabella was forced into exile and abdicated the throne in 1870.

The short-lived and chaotic First Republic (1873–74) was overthrown in a military coup and Isabella's 17-year-old son was placed on the throne as Alfonso XII. Unlike his mother, Alfonso was a strong ruler who worked hard to restore peace to the country after the chaos of the previous six years. He was popular with both the ruling elites and the majority of the Spanish people. However, in 1885, he died of tuberculosis. A few months later his infant son was proclaimed as **Alfonso XIII**.

Alfonso XIII displayed few of the political talents or the personal qualities of his father. Like Isabella, he showed little regard for constitutional government. Nor was he interested in tackling the social and economic problems facing Spain. He lived and worked within the rigid conventions of the Spanish court, changing his clothes several times a day but always preferring to be seen in military or naval uniforms.

The Church

The Spanish Catholic Church was strongly linked to the outlook and the policies of the ruling regime. By 1931 it had become hopelessly out of touch with developments and changes within the rest of the Church in Europe. Successive popes had worked since the 1880s to reconcile Catholicism with a changing and modernising world, and were directly addressing a range of fundamental social questions, especially the humane relationship that ought to exist between employers and their workers. The Spanish bishops ignored the Papacy's social policy, and remained identified with the interests of the industrialists and great landowners. This was perhaps unsurprising since the Spanish Church was phenomenally wealthy. In the 1830s the government confiscated Church lands and sold them off to existing landowners and the new industrial elite. As a result, the Church began to invest its money in new enterprises. It was believed that, by 1914, religious orders such as the Jesuits controlled one-third of the country's wealth and owned many industrial enterprises, including railways and banks. This wealth coined the Spanish saying 'El dinero es muy católica' ('Money is a good Catholic').

Glossary

Constitutional monarchy

A system of government in which the monarch shares political power with an elected parliament and government, similar to that of the UK.

Biography

Alfonso XIII

1886–1941

Alfonso XIII was king of Spain from the moment of his birth. He left Spain in April 1931, but never abdicated his throne. His fourth son was the father of King Juan Carlos I, who came to the throne in 1975 after the death of Francisco Franco. Alfonso favoured the Nationalists in the civil war, but Franco refused to accept him as king. Perhaps his only legacy is his patronage of several football clubs which adopted the name 'Real' (royal).

King Alfonso XIII in 1925

Glossary

Mass

The most important religious ceremony in the Catholic Church.

Anti-clericalism

Opposition to the involvement by the Church or the clergy in politics or public affairs.

Since the Church had forged such strong links with the monarchy and the landowners, it effectively lost its hold over the hearts and minds of most Spaniards. It still had some influence in the north of Spain, where the work of most priests was admired and valued. However, in the south of the country, the landless peasants had turned away from the influence of the Church. Many still used their local priest for the traditional punctuation marks in life of birth, marriage and death, but attendance at weekly **masses** was very low.

The Church maintained an obvious presence in towns and cities through its cathedrals and churches, but never gained the allegiance of industrial workers. There was a powerful tradition in Spain of **anti-clericalism**, which often exploded into attacks on Church property and the burning of churches and nunneries. But, despite the hostility shown by many Spaniards towards the Church, Spain's bishops made no real effort to reach out to workers and peasants. It was therefore unsurprising that the radical governments of 1931–33 passed many laws which reduced the Church's role in society, especially in education.

By 1931 it was clear that the bishops of the Catholic Church had set themselves firmly against any political, economic or social change within the country. It was thus almost inevitable that anti-clericalism would become one of the major themes running through the history of the Second Republic (1931–36).

The Church's role in education

The Catholic Church maintained almost complete control over the education of the young, and played a particularly powerful role in primary education. Most school teachers were practising Catholics, and local priests usually prescribed what was taught in both Church and state schools. A typical school day for most young pupils consisted of frequent prayer sessions and sewing, interspersed with talks on Church history and doctrine. It is surprising that, in a twentieth century European state, little attention was given to the teaching of reading; illiteracy rates were over 50% in most of Spain. Education in the rest of Western Europe was much more advanced.

There was also insufficient educational provision at secondary level, especially in the cities. Anti-clericals who opposed the Church's links with the traditional elites also campaigned for the ending of Catholicism's role in education.

The army

The army

The army were unpopular among the Spanish peasants and urban workers for many reasons. Upper and middle class recruits could avoid compulsory military service by buying an exemption. There were horrifically high non-combat casualty rates amongst soldiers overseas, especially in Cuba and Morocco. Many Spaniards also resented the role of the Civil Guard, which was attached to the military, in suppressing domestic protests.

The Church clearly played an important part in Spanish government and politics. **The army**, dominated by conservative and aristocratic officers, was another powerful representative of the existing elites in Spain. Like the Church, it was despised by most Spaniards. The armed forces had been unreformed for over a century and were disproportionately large for a country of just 24 million people. In 1914 there were 100,000 serving soldiers, along with an unusually large number of officers, some 12,000 in all, including nearly 300 generals (providing more than one officer for every ten soldiers). A quarter of the country's annual budget was used to fund the armed forces, and most of this was reserved for officers' pay.

Chapter 1: **Spain in 1931**

The army's support among some Spanish people declined rapidly from the late 1890s as a result of three key events.

- First, Spain was defeated in war by the United States in 1898. In the subsequent peace treaty, Spain was forced to cede Cuba, Puerto Rico and all its Pacific colonies, most notably the Philippines. Thus, at a time when other European powers were extending their own empires, Spain ceased to be an imperial power of any size.

- Second, the army's prestige was further damaged by the '**Tragic Week**' (*La Semana Trágica*) of 25 July–2 August 1909. During a week of disturbances and rioting in the Catalan capital Barcelona, armed forces opened fire on demonstrators, many of them anarchists (see below), killing 175 civilians. This violent confrontation resulted in the growth of forces opposed to the monarchy and the existing system of government.

- Third, Spanish forces were comprehensively defeated at the **battle of Annual** in 1921 against Rif tribesmen in Morocco. 10,000 Spanish troops were killed and 4000 taken prisoner. One week later, a further 7000 were killed in a separate incident.

By 1931 the Spanish army was without an effective role. The loss of the Pacific and Caribbean empires meant that troops were stationed either within Spain itself, where they served no real purpose, or in Morocco. Some officers, in both Spain and Morocco, began to reshape their idea of the army's role, not as the defender of empire but as the champion of the homeland against its enemies, both internal and external. It was the defence of traditional Spanish Catholic values, coupled with a militant anti-communism, that was to shape the ideas of the officer class from the 1920s onwards.

Challenges to the ruling elites

The anarchists

Widespread popular discontent found an outlet in the anarchist movement. Anarchism was a revolutionary philosophy which sought the violent overthrow of any system of central government. In its place, the anarchists intended to create a universal brotherhood of workers and peasants, which would co-operate in harmony at a local level without the need for a central government.

Anarchism had become increasingly popular ever since it was introduced into Spain in the 1860s. It was not well organised until 1910, when leading anarchists set up a trade union, the **CNT**. This became a powerful rival to the socialist trade union, the UGT, founded in 1888.

Anarchist groups were banned in the 1920s, but were to emerge as a major force during the Second Republic.

'Tragic Week': radical anti-clericalism

The growing anti-clericalism of some Spanish people was vividly demonstrated during the Barcelona riots by the burning of 22 churches and 34 convents.

Battle of Annual

Spanish troops in Spanish Morocco had been waging a constant struggle against local tribes since 1909. However, they were not well supplied with arms and their operations were not fully funded by Madrid. The losses sustained at Annual were the worst in recent Spanish history, and were a factor contributing to General Primo de Rivera's seizure of power.

CNT

The most powerful anarchist organisation, the National Confederation of Workers (*Confederación Nacional del Trabajo*), was very strong in Barcelona and throughout Andalusia. The CNT declared its membership at 1.58 million in 1934 against the 1.44 million members of the socialist UGT (*Unión General de Trabajadores*, the General Workers Union). The CNT was to play a vital role in both the Second Republic and the civil war.

9

Regional nationalists and separatists

Spain is a country which is divided, often by mountain ranges, into regions which are very different from each other. Two regions in particular developed their own culture and outlook, and caused problems for both the monarchy and the Second Republic.

The Basque Country is in the north of Spain and borders France. Surrounded by mountains, it has maintained its own culture and its inhabitants speak Basque, one of the oldest languages in Europe. Basque nationalism developed in the early twentieth century, though it was repressed by both the monarchy and the dictatorship of Primo de Rivera.

In the north-east of Spain lies the rich and diverse region of Catalonia. Like the Basque Country, Catalonia possesses its own language, and has a long tradition of resisting control from Madrid. From 1900, a separatist political party, the Lliga, made increasing demands for regional self-government.

Such regional differences complicated Spanish government. During the Great War of 1914–18, the Basque Country and Catalonia had both boomed. Basque steel mills and the Catalonian textile industries had supplied materials to armies on both sides of the war. However, the central government threatened to impose heavy taxes on both regions. As a result, the middle-class factory owners in these regions united with dissatisfied workers, demanding either greater autonomy or complete independence from Spain.

The end of the Spanish monarchy, 1931

Although Spain was a constitutional monarchy, Alfonso XIII preferred to work with the military elite rather than the politicians, and he was in almost constant conflict with successive governments. He never won the affection of his people and, throughout his reign, he displayed no real understanding of, nor any real interest in tackling, Spain's pressing social and economic problems.

Alfonso had a strong attachment to the Catholic Church. When he visited Pope Pius XI in 1923, he declared that he was the first truly Catholic king of Spain in centuries who was ready to shed his own blood for the Church. This demonstrates just how out of touch he had become from Spain and its problems.

Opposition to Alfonso personally, and to the institution of monarchy in general, developed rapidly in the 1920s. The king gave his support to **General Primo de Rivera**, who overthrew the constitutional government in September 1923 and instituted a dictatorship which lasted until 1930. Although Primo de Rivera's dictatorship ended in 1930, the king did not restore constitutional rule, but appointed another military government.

By 1931 the monarchy had become identified with military rule and the destruction of Spain's constitutional forms of government. When the government held local elections in April of that year, the massive Republican and Socialist gains demonstrated how far the monarchy had lost the confidence of the people. As the Second Republic was proclaimed, Alfonso XIII left the country. Few mourned his departure.

Biography

General Miguel Primo de Rivera

(1870–1930)

Primo de Rivera seized power in September 1923, following a wave of violence and domestic military intervention that had built up in Spain from 1919. His regime was both popular and successful in its early years. Conditions for urban workers improved as the government increased spending on education and health, and provided employment through an ambitious public works programme. The Moroccan war ended when Spanish forces defeated Abd-el-Krim in 1926. After 1925, the regime lost much of its early popularity as the economy began to slow down and unemployment rose. The world slump of 1929 devastated Spain's economy; exports dropped dramatically and the peseta lost over 30% of its value. As landowners, industrialists and even the king began to distance themselves from the dictator, he resigned in January 1930. He died two months later in Paris.

Conclusion: How divided was Spanish society in 1931?

Spain was clearly a divided nation in 1931, but the divisions were quite complex. There were serious tensions between the central government and growing demands for self-rule, especially in Catalonia. The Spanish Catholic Church and the army faced an array of enemies determined to reduce their powers dramatically. Above all, perhaps, the divisions between rich and poor, in the cities and the countryside, were deep and bitter. It was these problems which the Second Republic would have to address, and to tackle with urgency.

Activity: Problems facing Spain in 1931

Write a report for the new Republican government of 1931 on the problems which they have inherited in the following areas:

- the economy
- education
- the Catholic Church
- the army.

Identify the single most important problem, and suggest possible solutions.

Activity: Flight of the monarchy

Make a list of the key groups within Spanish society in 1931. Write a short diary entry announcing the departure of Alfonso XIII from the perspective of a member of each group, making clear their feelings on the news.

Which groups would welcome the king's departure?

Read out your entries and discuss your reasoning. Invite your friends to leave one-sentence 'comments' indicating whether they agree or disagree, and why.

Taking it further

You can find further information on anarchists and socialists in Paul Preston's *A Concise History of the Spanish Civil War* (1996).

Chapter 2: **The years of reform, 1931–33**

Key questions

- Why did the Conservative and Radical Republican parties leave the government so quickly?
- How successful were the government's agrarian reforms?
- What did the anti-clerical laws achieve?

There was widespread enthusiasm for the Second Republic, referred to by many as *'La Niña Bonita'* – the beautiful girl. Elections in June 1931 showed overwhelming support for the parties loyal to the Republic. However, this unity among Spaniards was short-lived. By 1933, the traditional conservative forces in Spanish society were horrified by the government's attacks on their vested interests. They vigorously opposed the reforms which tackled the Church, the army and the land. Equally, there was increasing unrest among the workers in the cities and the landless labourers in the countryside: both these groups felt that the pace of change was too slow. By September 1933, the government of Manuel Azaña appeared to have run out of reforming zeal and President Alcalá Zamora called for fresh elections.

Biography

Niceto Alcalá Zamora

1877–1949

Alcalá Zamora became the first Prime Minister of the new Republic. He was a landowner from Cordoba, and had served as a minister during the time of the monarchy. A devout Catholic and a firm conservative, he resigned in October 1931 in protest over the government's proposed religious reforms. In December 1931, he was elected President of the Republic and he held the office until he was forced to resign in April 1936 for behaving unconstitutionally, a few months before the outbreak of the civil war. Although he was essentially loyal to the Republic, he soon gained a reputation for meddling in the affairs of government.

Timeline

April 1931	The Provisional Government took power
April–June 1931	Land, employment and army reforms introduced
June 1931	Elections for the Constituent Cortes
August–December 1931	Debates on the constitution
October 1931	Manuel Azaña appointed Prime Minister
January 1932	Castilblanco and Arnedo killings
August 1932	General Sanjurjo's attempted coup
September 1932	Catalan Statute and Agrarian Reform Law passed
January 1933	Casas Viejas massacre
September 1933	Azaña dismissed: elections called for November

Take note

As you work through this chapter, consider to what extent each of the government's reforms was successful. Use the information you gather to complete the following diagram:

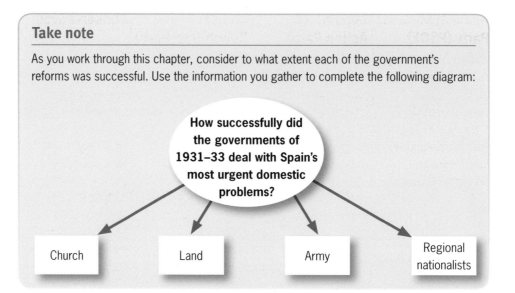

How successfully did the governments of 1931–33 deal with Spain's most urgent domestic problems?

Church   Land   Army   Regional nationalists

The Provisional Government

As Alfonso XIII left the country on 14 April 1931, a revolutionary committee formed in **San Sebastian** the previous August took over the running of the country as a provisional government. The **Provisional Government** was to govern Spain until a new constitutuion had been agreed.

The Provisional Government of 1931 was a coalition. In May 2010, a coalition government took office in Britain. It consisted of representatives from just two parties, the Conservatives and the Liberal Democrats. Its leaders were able to agree a joint programme very quickly. In Spain, however, the Provisional Government drew its membership chiefly from four parties which spanned the whole political spectrum from left to right. These parties had agreed in 1930 on just one policy: the ending of the Spanish monarchy. Once this had been achieved, the divisions between the parties became more apparent and the grand coalition soon began to break up. In October, the Conservatives, under their leader **Niceto Alcalá Zamora**, withdrew their support for the government in protest at its anti-clerical programme. In December, the Radical Republicans were excluded from government by the new Prime Minister, **Manuel Azaña**.

Biography

Manuel Azaña

1880–1940

Azaña was a lawyer and writer who had been an active republican for many years. He became Minister of War in 1931 and succeeded Alcalá Zamora as Prime Minister in October that year. The leader of the middle-class progressives, and an immensely talented politician and speaker, he was regarded by many Spaniards as 'the strong man of the Republic'. He earned the determined opposition of the right because of his fierce anti-clericalism.

Left wing ← Centre → Right wing

Spanish Socialist Party (PSOE)	Republican Action Party	Radical Republican Party	Conservatives
Wanted radical social change in the interests of workers and landless peasants Strongly anti-clerical Main representative: Largo Caballero, Minister of Labour	Liberal reformers Strongly anti-clerical Mostly middle class Main representative: Manuel Azaña, Minister of War 1931, Prime Minister 1931–33	Despite its name, a party which represented the interests of the middle classes Alarmed by the radicalism of the Socialists The main governing party in the years 1934–36 Main representative: Alejandro Lerroux	Wanted to continue the pre-1931 system of government, but without the monarchy Represented the interests of major landowners, the army and, most of all, the Catholic Church Main representative: Niceto Alcalá Zamora, Prime Minister 1931, President 1931–36

Main political parties in Spain, 1931

Pact of San Sebastian, 1930

In August 1930, a meeting led by Niceto Alcalá Zamora was held in San Sebastian in northern Spain. It was attended by representatives of most Republican groups, who agreed to form a revolutionary committee which aimed to end the Spanish monarchy. They were united by their republicanism but found little other common ground.

The Government

Provisional Government A temporary government which governed Spain until a new constitution had been agreed.
Constitution A system of rules which lays down how a country is to be governed.
Cortes A single chamber consisting of elected representatives of the Spanish people, similar to the British House of Commons. All laws had to be approved by the Cortes before they could come into effect.
President The head of the Spanish state. The President had little real power, though Alcalá Zamora interfered in government affairs while he was President (December 1931–April 1936).
Prime Minister The President appointed the Prime Minister, who was head of the government.

Glossary

Constituent Cortes

The Constituent Cortes was elected to perform just one task – to draw up and approve a constitution for the Second Republic. Once it had completed this task, it was supposed to dissolve itself. However, by general agreement, it continued to function as the parliament of the country until the elections of 1933.

The Republic was born during the worst years of the Great Depression. Overall industrial production shrank. In March 1936, Spanish industry was only producing 77% of its 1929 output. Production of iron fell by a third between 1930 and 1935, and the production of other metals such as zinc, silver and copper halved. The value of Spanish stocks and shares also dropped significantly so, by 1935, the market was worth only 63% of its 1929 value. While production fell, unemployment rose, from 400,000 at the end of 1931 to 600,000 two years later. Government revenue thus fell at a time when the Republic urgently needed funds to finance its reform programme, and this would affect the success of most of the reforms of the years 1931–33.

The new government thus faced a daunting number of problems, which ministers believed required rapid, and in some cases, drastic action. However, their enthusiasm for change was not shared by all Spaniards. While most workers and agricultural labourers hoped for speedy and dramatic improvements in their living and working conditions, right-wing forces did their utmost to resist any measures which would transform Spanish society.

The Constitution of the Second Republic, December 1931

The most pressing tasks for the new government were to call elections for a **Constituent Cortes** and to establish a new constitution. **The elections** were held in June, and the Spanish voters gave overwhelming support to the new Republic. The Socialists won 115 seats and became the largest party in the Cortes. The right-wing groups had not expected the fall of the monarchy and their disorganisation was reflected in the fact that they took barely 50 seats. The parties supporting the government had a massive majority of seats.

Debates on the creation of a constitution for the new Republic began in August and the final version was agreed in December. Some of its terms worried the Conservatives. The influence of the left on the government was apparent by the description of Spain as 'a democratic republic of workers of all kinds'. Women received the vote for the first time and a number of anti-clerical provisions restricted the rights of the Catholic Church. Many moderate and conservative Spaniards who had supported the Republic now became concerned at the radical direction which the government was taking.

June 1931 election

Supporting the government:

365 deputies

Socialists: 115 seats

Left-wing Republicans combined: 150 seats

Radical Republicans: 90 seats

Conservatives: 10 seats

Opposing the government: 50 deputies

Anti-Republican groups: 50 seats (including 20 Monarchists)

The Second Republic

Early reforms

Army reforms

The Minister of War, Manuel Azaña, moved speedily to tackle over-manning in the army. He announced that all officers would be allowed to transfer to the reserve list on full pay (in effect retiring from the army). This was an unusually generous offer, which was taken up by some 8,000 officers. Azaña also tried to reduce the size of the military budget by cutting the period of military service to one year and by closing the military academy at Saragossa.

These measures did not improve the efficiency of the armed forces, nor did they increase the doubtful loyalty shown by officers towards the Republic.

Reducing the size of the officer class inevitably closed up several avenues of promotion for junior officers, who would express their disillusion by flocking to the Nationalist cause in 1936. Moreover, **Francisco Franco** had been the commanding officer at the Saragossa Military Academy since 1927. Here he had instilled into young officers his belief that the army was Spain's most powerful protector against both external and domestic enemies. His farewell address to the cadets was, unsurprisingly, deliberately insulting towards Azaña.

Biography

Francisco Franco

1892–1975

Son of a naval postmaster, Franco graduated from the Toledo Military Academy in 1910. Although a small man, he proved to be a brave and able officer, rising rapidly through the ranks. In 1928 he was appointed commander of Spain's new military academy at Saragossa, in which role he visited academies in both France and Germany. Franco supported the military dictatorship of Primo de Rivera and was considered a threat to the new regime in 1931. His role in the civil war and subsequent dictatorship proved them right.

Agrarian reforms

The Minister of Labour, the Socialist **Francisco Largo Caballero**, issued a number of decrees between April and July 1931 which were designed to address the most pressing problems that faced agrarian workers, especially in the south of the country. He established an eight-hour day for agricultural labourers, thus introducing overtime pay for the first time in the countryside. Wage disputes were to be settled by mixed committees of labourers and landowners. The rights of small tenant farmers were protected to ensure that they could not be evicted from their farms without good cause.

The most significant reform on agricultural employment was the Law of Municipal Boundaries of May 1931. This required landowners to offer jobs to those living within their municipality before importing migrant workers. This practice was common in the countryside because it enabled landowners to keep wages low as well as neutralising the effectiveness of any local strikes.

Taken together, the decrees on agriculture had a dramatic effect on the rights of both landowners and peasants. The balance of power in the countryside had shifted decisively towards agricultural workers, who flocked to join the FNTT, the agricultural section of the socialist union, the **UGT**. For their part, the landowners did their best to thwart the decrees and were often successful in evading them completely. The bitter hostility which the southern landowners developed towards the Republic helped to fuel the growth of right-wing and conservative parties over the next few years.

Church-state relations

Of all the problems which the government faced, the relations between the Spanish state and the Catholic Church proved to be the most divisive. Apart from the Conservatives, the diverse parties which made up the Provisional Government were united by a strong and aggressive anti-clericalism.

Biography

Francisco Largo Caballero

1869–1946

In 1925, Largo Caballero became head of the Spanish Socialist Party (PSOE) and of its union, the UGT. When a right-wing government came to power in Spain in 1933, his attitudes shifted dramatically leftwards and he took up the views of the more extreme socialists who aimed at a violent revolution. He held the office of Prime Minister for a short period during the civil war (September 1936–May 1937).

Prime Minister Largo Caballero, c.1930s

UGT

The *Unión General de Trabajadores* (General Workers' Union) was founded in 1888. It grew rapidly during the Second Republic, largely because of the large number of agricultural workers who joined it.

The Church had been a powerful supporter of both the monarchy and the dictatorship of Primo de Rivera, and was naturally viewed as a massive obstacle to progress and social change. Shortly after the Republic was proclaimed, the pope indicated to Spanish bishops that they should respect and obey the new government, but his advice went largely unheeded. In May 1931 **Cardinal Segura**, the leader of Spain's Roman Catholics, issued a strongly-worded letter in which he urged Catholics to vote against government parties in the forthcoming elections. There was an immediate reaction to his statement. He was expelled from the country and, in a separate development, crowds burned down churches in Madrid and in other cities.

It was in this context that the government and the Constituent Cortes discussed the religious clauses proposed in the constitution. Articles 26 and 27 separated Church and state, provided for the closure of all religious schools and threatened to phase out the state subsidy to the clergy over the next two years.

While these attacks on the Church might appear understandable in the context of the time, they were at best unwise and at worst self-defeating. On a national level, the country simply could not afford to build, equip and staff thousands of new schools to replace the Church schools and their teachers. Articles 26 and 27 encouraged local councils to take a spiteful and petty attitude to the Church. In many towns and villages, religious processions were banned, the ringing of church bells was prohibited and priests were sometimes forced to remove religious sculptures from the outside of their churches. Many ordinary parish priests, often barely better off than their parishioners, had supported the establishment of the Republic, and they relied on the state subsidy to provide them with most of their income. Its threatened removal over the next two years, coupled with the open hostility of local authorities, was to alienate the clergy from the Republic and was instrumental in fostering the creation of an alliance of right-wing Catholic parties by 1933.

Glossary

Agrarian
Relating to agricultural or rural matters.

Autonomy
The right to self-government granted to one or more regions of a country.

Developing problems

Changes in the government, October 1931
The government's attacks on the Church caused a major political crisis in October 1931. The Prime Minister and the Minister for Home Affairs, both Conservatives and devout Catholics, resigned in protest. Their presence within the government had reassured the right; their departure made the government appear even more radical. The new government depended on the support of left-wing groups and parties in order to pass its reforming programme. Azaña's government was determined to carry out two significant reforms: a major **agrarian** reform and the granting of **autonomy** to Catalonia.

The Agrarian Reform Law, 1932
Largo Caballero had already addressed the most pressing agrarian problems in 1931; the government now sought to build on these reforms. They aimed at nothing less than a comprehensive programme of land redistribution to meet the needs of peasants and tenant farmers in central and southern Spain. This policy ignored the small farmers in the north of the country, most of whom had to work as well as farm in order to survive.

The reform which was finally enacted horrified major landowners. An Institute of Agrarian Reform was set up to tackle the land question. Any estate of more than 23 hectares could be taken over, and could subsequently be used to resettle farmers on smallholdings of sufficient size to provide a decent income. Although this seemed to be a highly radical scheme, the reform turned out to be meaningless. The Institute never had sufficient funds to buy out the landowners and in its first year of activity it resettled only a few thousand families.

The failure of the government's agrarian reforms had long-term implications for its survival. Members of the agricultural union, the FNTT, were dismayed at the government's apparent inability to respond to their grievances. This was to encourage growing opposition among the Socialists and within the UGT as a whole towards the moderate and insufficient reforms carried out by the government.

The Catalan Statute, 1932

Many British people know just two things about Catalonia: the sandy beaches of the Costa Brava and the sporting prowess of FC Barcelona. Catalonia is much more than this. It possesses its own individual and cosmopolitan culture, less Spanish than Mediterranean, thanks to its long traditions of international trade. Most Catalans speak their own language – Catalan – rather than Spanish. Economic development since the late nineteenth century made the region one of the wealthiest and most industrialised regions of Spain.

Catalonia was harshly treated during the dictatorship of Primo de Rivera. Many features of Catalan culture were suppressed and the modest powers of home rule which had been conceded were revoked. These actions only served to boost Catalan nationalism and, in 1931, most of the region's population expected the Madrid government to agree to their demands for increased autonomy. In a **plebiscite** in that year, over 99% of the votes cast were in favour of sweeping powers of self-government. The Catalan Statute of 1932 **devolved** considerable powers in domestic affairs to a Catalan parliament in Barcelona.

This reform meant that the Republic gained the overwhelming support of a whole region of Spain, apart from a small number of opponents drawn mostly from the middle classes. Within a wider context, however, Catalan autonomy was viewed by Spanish nationalists, and crucially by the army, as undermining the unity and integrity of the whole country. And no such accomodation was reached with the Basque separatists, fostering tensions there.

Repression and unrest

The Second Republic faced opposition from the very outset, from both the left and the right of the political spectrum. The anarchist trade union, the CNT, was vigorously opposed to what it perceived as a middle-class government which ruled in the interests of the few and not the many. It was prepared to foster strikes, in cities and in the countryside, aimed at promoting a national revolution. The forces of the right were not as well organised, but developed into an opposing force which was at least as strong as that created by the left.

Glossary
Plebiscite
When the whole electorate of a country or region vote to decide on a single question of importance.
Devolve
To transfer clearly specified powers from a central government to a regional government.

Civil Guard and Assault Guard

There were two paramilitary police forces active within Republican Spain:
The elite Civil Guard of roughly 70,000 men, were used largely to maintain order in the countryside, where they usually sided with the landowners against the peasants.
Known as the *asaltos*, the Assault Guard were a newly formed Republican force which policed the towns and cities, and numbered around 30,000.

Biography

General José Sanjurjo

(1872–1936)

Sanjurjo served in the Spanish army in Cuba in the 1890s and in Morocco in the early 1920s. In 1928 Alfonso XIII appointed him as a commander in the Civil Guard. Sanjurjo welcomed the Second Republic, but fell out with Azaña, who blamed him (wrongly) for the deaths at Castilblanco and Arnedo and secured his dismissal. Imprisoned in 1932 after his attempted rising, he was freed in 1934 and went into exile in Portugal. In May 1936 Sanjurjo joined forces with Franco, Mola and de Llano in the plot to overthrow the Republic. He intended to fly back to Spain, but his plane crashed and he was killed. The pilot blamed the crash on the heavy luggage of impressive uniforms which Sanjurjo insisted on accompanying him.

The government's response to unrest was surprisingly harsh and reminded many Spaniards of the repressive policies of the monarchy. A CNT-inspired strike of telephone workers took place in July 1931, largely in protest at foreign involvement in Spain's telephone system. The government called out the army and the **Civil Guard**, which destroyed the strike with unnecessary violence, killing 30 strikers.

Further evidence of Civil Guard brutality occured at the end of 1931. A Socialist strike in the province of Badajoz inspired the peasants of the tiny village of Castilblanco. The four Civil Guards garrisoned in the village tried to ban a meeting in the village square, but were attacked and killed by the crowd. A few days later, the Civil Guard opened fire on striking workers in the town of Arnedo in the north of the country, killing 11 people, including women and children.

Most Spaniards deplored the Civil Guards' ferocious behaviour, and blamed the government for the many deaths and injuries suffered by largely innocent people. The government placed responsibility on the Guards' commander, **General Sanjurjo**, who was dismissed. For a brief period, Sanjurjo posed a threat to the Republic's stability. He was opposed to Azaña's military reforms and, like many army officers, resisted the granting of autonomy to Catalonia. In August 1932 he proclaimed an uprising, not against the Republic itself, but against the current government. The attempted coup was a miserable failure, and Sanjurjo was captured and imprisoned. However, the easy defeat of the rising energised the supporters of the Republic, and helped speed up the passing of the Catalan Statute and the Agrarian Reform Law.

Spain's military elite, including Sanjurjo and Franco, with Primo de Rivera in October 1925

Casas Viejas, 1933

The farmers in the town of Casas Viejas were angry at the slow pace of agrarian reform and, inspired by CNT action elsewhere in Spain, rose against the Republic in January 1933. They attacked the local barracks of the Civil Guard, killing several of their number. Retribution was rapid and severe. Reinforcements were sent to the town, including members of the **Assault Guard**, which had been formed to counter urban violence. Armed with light artillery and machine guns, they were determined to wipe out resistance.

20 prisoners were shot in cold blood, some of them after prolonged periods of torture. Houses were set on fire, including that of the anarchist ringleader, known as 'Six Fingers', and many people were burned alive.

The effects of the Casas Viejas massacre were lasting and profound. It seriously discredited Azaña's government and was a major factor in its fall in late 1933. Most of the working class, and the landless peasants, had been strong supporters of the Republic from the outset; they now became increasingly bitter and disillusioned. The right saw in this affair the opportunity to develop a successful propaganda campaign against the government, and to bring together right-wing forces into a single group with the aim of taking power at the next elections. These could not be delayed for long. In the autumn of 1933, after the Socialists abandoned their policy of co-operation with the Republicans, President Alcalá Zamora dismissed the government. Fresh elections to the Cortes were called for November 1933.

The dead lie in piles after Casas Viejas

Successes of the Second Republic

It would be easy to consider the whole period 1931–36 as leading inevitably to the civil war that broke out in July 1936. This is perhaps a mistaken view to take. If we look at the government of 1931–33 in its own right, and without any reference to subsequent events, we can see that it had substantial achievements to its credit.

- All Spaniards were granted a wide range of civil and political rights, including the granting of the vote to all women. The laws on civil marriage and divorce, which were protected by the constitution, were the most advanced in Europe at the time.

- Workers in industry were granted an eight-hour day, along with other benefits such as paid holidays.

- A massive programme of school building was begun.

- The rights of agricultural workers were strengthened, including security of tenure for tenant farmers and increased wages for landless labourers.

- Despite its limitations, the Agrarian Reform Law did attempt to tackle the land question.

- There was some attempt to tackle over-manning within the armed forces.

- The position of the Catholic Church within Spanish life was severely restricted, and a start was made on educational reform.

- Perhaps the government's greatest success was the Catalan Statute, which settled a long-standing grievance and encouraged most Catalonians to give strong support to the Republic.

Taking it further

A detailed assessment of the successes and failures of the Second Republic can be found in Francisco J. Romero Salvadó, *Twentieth-Century Spain, 1898–1998* (1999).

Conclusion: How far were the actions of the Republican government mistaken?

The Republic faced many pressing problems when it came to power. Economic depression and high spending had left the government with little money to fund urgent reforms, and this helps to explain the failure of the Agrarian Reform Law, which was not supported with sufficient funds to tackle successfully the question of land reform. Ministers might have been able to increase government revenue by increasing taxes on more wealthy Spaniards, but they were not prepared to take such action.

The government's fierce attacks on the Catholic Church were ill-advised and mistaken. In April 1931, most Catholics were prepared to support the Republic but they were shocked by the local attacks on their grassroots religion and they were upset that anti-clericalism had been written into the constitution, the basic law of the Second Republic. The Church's response was to support the creation of right-wing Catholic groups which aimed to reverse all the government's anti-clerical laws.

However, the government's greatest mistake was its failure to appreciate just what had happened in April 1931. The monarchy had vanished, but there remained the vastly powerful traditional conservative forces which had sustained it for so long. The government made no real attempt to compromise with these forces. On the contrary, ministers behaved as if they would be in power for many years, and ignored the legitimate fears and concerns of many Spaniards. Thus there developed an organised right-wing opposition consisting of major landowners, army officers and the Catholic Church. Over the next few years, they were to play havoc with the hard-won reforms of 1931–33.

Activity: Successes and failures of the Second Republic

- Using your notes from this chapter, draw up a review of the governments of 1931–33, looking at the key areas of reform and rating their success.

- Write a speech to address the Spanish Cortes arguing either for more time for the reformers or for a change of government based on your review.

- Write a newspaper article summarising the problems faced by whoever takes over in November 1933 and giving advice, from the point of view of either a left-wing or right-wing observer.

- Draw up an action plan with which to brief the new government.

Activity: Azaña's speech

In a speech to the Constituent Cortes in August 1931, Azaña declared that 'Spain has ceased to be Catholic'. Revisit the information on the Church in Chapter 1. To what extent was Azaña's claim justified? How might Catholics react to his statement?

Chapter 3: **The years of reaction, 1934–36**

Key questions

- How far did the governments of 1934–36 roll back the reforms of 1931–33?
- How successful was the CEDA in fulfilling the aims of its supporters?
- To what extent did Spanish politics become increasingly divided in the years 1934–36?

The *Bienio Negro*, or the 'Two Black Years', is the term used by the Spanish Left to describe the years 1934–35, when the CEDA and their Radical Republican allies rolled back most of the reforms passed in the years 1931–33. This period of right-wing reaction sparked the most violent anti-government rebellion of the whole Second Republic period, the Asturias rising of 1934. The suppression of the rising, and its aftermath, only deepened the gulf between left and right in Spain. By early 1936, the polarisation of politics had gone so far that many Spaniards were convinced that the democratic experiment embarked on in 1931 with such high expectations was on the verge of collapse.

Timeline

February 1933	CEDA formed
November 1933	Elections to the Cortes held. Triumph of the right
December 1933	Largest CNT insurrection
May 1934	Law of Municipal Boundaries repealed
June 1934	FNTT land-workers strike
October 1934	The Asturias rising
May 1935	Gil Robles appointed Minister of War. He then appointed Franco as Chief of the General Staff
January 1936	Cortes dissolved and elections called for 16 February. Popular Front established

Take note

List, in order of importance, the factors which led to the CEDA's success and the Socialists' defeat in the elections of November 1933.

The reactionary right

The reactionary right refers to parties and politicians who were opposed to significant social or political change. The Spanish reactionary right intended to reverse or neutralise most of the radical reforms of the Azaña government. These policies would inevitably lead to clashes with the left-wing parties, who wanted to continue the reforms of 1931–33.

The CEDA

The most important political development of 1933 was the formation of the CEDA – the Spanish Confederation of the Autonomous Right (*Confederación Española de Derechas Autónomas*).

During the early months of the Second Republic, the traditional and right-wing forces in the country had been disorganised and ineffective. They were tainted by their association with the monarchy, and their poor showing in the 1931 election allowed the reforming parties to rule unchallenged for over two years.

Jose Maria Gil Robles

1898–1980

Elected to the Constituent Cortes in 1931, Gil Robles led the CEDA from 1933. As Minister of War in 1935, he was responsible for appointing Franco as Chief of the General Staff. He dissolved the CEDA in 1937 and played no part in the events of the civil war or the Franco dictatorship.

Gil Robles in 1932

November 1933 election

Supporting the government:
309 deputies
The CEDA: 115 seats
Radical Republicans: 104 seats
Other centre-right parties: 90 seats
Opposing the government:
124 deputies
Socialists: 58 seats
Regional parties: 47 seats
Republican Action Party (Azaña's party): 7 seats
Other left-wing parties: 12 seats (including one Communist)

Right-wing and Catholic forces were dismayed by the constitution, the government's anti-clericalism, and the attacks on the privileges of the army and the landowning class. Following the dissolution of the monarchy, *Acción Popular* had been established as a party which represented the interests of the Catholic Church. However, the leader of *Acción Popular*, **José Maria Gil Robles**, became increasingly aware that the party would never be strong enough to challenge the power of the left. He worked on developing a broad coalition of right-wing parties which would fight the next election as a single group and mount a powerful onslaught on the government and the ruling parties.

As a result, the CEDA was formed in February 1933. This was an umbrella organisation for a number of right-wing, largely Catholic, parties and groups. CEDA was formed with the declared aim of defending religion, property and, above all, the unity of Spain. Its members refused to confirm their loyalty to the Republic. It was given substantial financial support by landowners and industrialists, which made it likely that it would reverse or at least water down the social and agrarian reforms promoted by Azaña's government.

Gil Robles' own political views were a source of debate in the 1930s, and are still discussed by historians today. It was unclear whether he accepted the idea of democracy, especially as he refused to declare his loyalty to the Republic and its institutions. He had visited Germany and Italy, and was impressed by the strength of each country's fascist dictatorship. He also became aware of the power of propaganda in gaining wide support, and used it very effectively in the elections of 1933 and 1936. The left were convinced that, if Gil Robles and the CEDA gained power, they would proceed to dismantle the Republic and replace it with a more authoritarian form of government, possibly a dictatorship similar to that of Primo de Rivera in the 1920s. It was this suspicion of Gil Robles' intentions that earned him and his party the strong opposition of President Alcalá Zamora.

The election of November 1933

In November 1933 the electoral system was changed, with large constituencies electing several members. This system favoured wide electoral coalitions and worked against parties which stood independently. The Socialist Party, which had dominated the Constituent Cortes, made a catastrophic error when it decided to fight the **1933 election** alone. Although it still gained a large number of votes, it halved its representation in the Cortes, falling back to 58 deputies. Azaña's Republican Action Party, with just seven deputies, was virtually destroyed as an effective force. The two big winners in the election were **Lerroux's** Radical Republicans, with 104 seats, and the CEDA, whose 115 deputies made it the largest party in the Cortes. The losers were, without doubt, the Socialist Party and the moderate parties of the centre. The latter saw their support drain away as Spanish politics became increasingly polarised. Women voted for the first time in this election. Although they voted in large numbers for the right-wing parties, their votes alone cannot explain the right's success.

If electoral arithmetic were the only consideration, then the CEDA would have been invited to form a government. However, President Alcalá Zamora, who increasingly saw his role as that of the Republic's defender, refused to appoint Gil Robles as Prime Minister. Instead, Lerroux formed a government drawn largely from the Radical Republicans, with broad CEDA support. The two parties would now work together to undo many of the reforms of 1931–33.

Government policies, 1934

The Radical Republicans had long been regarded by their opponents as a group of opportunists who shared no deeply held political views; the governments of 1934–35 simply confirmed this opinion. Prompted by the CEDA, they ignored or reversed almost all the reforms achieved since 1931. Although Lerroux was personally hostile to Catholicism, anti-clerical legislation was abandoned; in particular, the education budget was cut and religious schools were allowed to continue to operate. Laws which protected industrial and agricultural workers were largely repealed, leading to immediate and substantial cuts in wages. Most importantly, the mild reforms undertaken in the countryside were abolished. The large landowners' reward for the financial support they gave to the CEDA came in the form of the curtailing of peasants' rights and the eviction of those who had settled on confiscated land. The repeal of the Law of Municipal Boundaries was followed by a general strike organised by the FNTT, which was easily crushed by the Civil Guard. The triumph of the landed gentry was summed up in their advice to hungry agrarian labourers: '*comed República*' (let the Republic feed you).

Left-wing resistance

The constant demands which Gil Robles made of the government in 1934 led to frequent Cabinet reshuffles, though Alcalá Zamora remained determined to keep CEDA deputies out of office. In October, however, the President finally gave way and agreed to a new government headed by Lerroux which included three CEDA ministers in minor positions. This change in policy was to have devastating results.

Ever since its founding in 1879, the Socialist Party had operated as a constitutional party, rather than a revolutionary organisation. The party had worked with Azaña between 1931 and 1933 in carrying out a major programme of reform, and in influencing the final form of the Second Republic's constitution. However, the limited nature of the reforms, especially those that tried to improve the lot of the landless agricultural labourers, frustrated Largo Caballero and the members of his party. They were also suspicious of the ultimate ambitions of Gil Robles and the CEDA, and feared that Spain could be transformed into a fascist dictatorship on Italian or German lines. These concerns caused a major shift in Socialist thinking in 1934. Prompted by Largo Caballero, the Socialist Party developed a policy which envisaged the creation of a people's democracy, not through the ballot box, but by an armed uprising. Throughout 1934 Largo Caballero warned of such an eventuality if the CEDA ever entered government.

Biography

Alejandro Lerroux

(1864–1947)

Lerroux established a powerful political base in Barcelona in the 1900s, where his profoundly anti-clerical outlook was very popular. He formed the Radical Republican Party in 1908, and was a member of the Pact of San Sebastian in 1930. He was appointed Prime Minister three times in the years 1933–35. Lerroux and his supporters had few political principles, and used power to support their own personal and financial interests.

Alejandro Lerroux

The formation of the new government in October triggered that revolt. The rising that followed was organised in two parts of the country. In Catalonia, the rebellion was badly organised and planned by nationalists and was easily put down by government troops. The Asturias rising proved to be an entirely different affair.

The Asturias rising, October 1934

Parts of Asturias were among the most industrialised areas of Spain in the 1930s, and the local economy relied very heavily on the coal mining industry. The world recession had led to a slump in demand for coal, and mine owners responded by slashing wages and sacking workers. 70% of the region's workers were members of trade unions, most belonging to the socialist UGT and were therefore well organised long before the rising took place. The Socialist Party's drift away from democratic methods towards a revolutionary standpoint led to socialist youth groups arming themselves and undergoing military training in the region's mountainous areas. All the left-wing groups in Asturias, including the Communists, sank their differences and co-operated with each other, which had not happened in Catalonia. This co-operation made the rising difficult to suppress, and turned it into a virtual dress rehearsal for the civil war which broke out in 1936.

The rising, planned for several months, broke out on 5 October. Within a few days the rebels had attacked and neutralised Civil Guard posts and established control over most of the province. The government in Madrid sent substantial forces into Asturias. At least 20,000 government troops marched on the province, most of them Moorish and Foreign Legion forces shipped over from Africa. They were supported by the Spanish Navy, which shelled the coastal cities, and the air force, which bombed towns and villages indiscriminately. Although General Lopez Ochoa was nominally in charge of the operation, he took his orders directly from General Franco in Madrid.

The rebels' resistance was broken in two weeks of vicious combat, and was followed by savage reprisals and widespread atrocities. The hospital in the region's capital of Oviedo was full of wounded from both sides; many were shot without cause. Whole villages were razed to the ground, and torture and execution without trial were commonplace. In the aftermath of the rising, trade unionists were dismissed *en masse* from their jobs, and thousands were imprisoned. Perhaps as many as 2000 people were killed in the Asturias rising, with a further 7000 wounded.

While many Spaniards saw the Asturias rising as a heroic action which was doomed to failure, others regarded the Socialist Party's action as totally irresponsible. The election of 1933 had shown the growing polarisation of politics and society, and the rising had the effect of forcing many moderate Spaniards further to the political right. A worrying development was the way in which the rising was reported in the right-wing press. Atrocity stories were commonplace. There were stories of the widespread rape and murder of nuns, of priests being burned alive or hanged from meathooks, and even that 20 sons and daughters of policemen had their eyes put out. Evidence of these atrocities was never found, but they served their purpose of terrifying the middle classes. Such stories were to be used again and again during the civil war.

The aftermath of street fighting in Asturias

Azaña and the reorganisation of the left, 1935

The Asturias rising provided some useful lessons for the left to reflect on. Although the rising had ultimately failed, its initial success demonstrated that left-wing parties and unions could be successful as long as they were prepared to work with, rather than against, each other. The subsequent formation of such an alliance at a national level was almost entirely down to the work of Manuel Azaña.

Azaña played no part in the 1934 risings, but nonetheless was imprisoned for a few months afterwards (he had shown that he was willing to become President if the revolt succeeded). This served only to increase his personal prestige as the 'strong man of the Republic'. He was convinced that there should be 'no enemies on the left', and throughout 1935 worked tirelessly in negotiating with left-wing leaders. He pointed out that disunity had proved disastrous in the 1933 elections, and that a united coalition had brought substantial success to the CEDA and its allies. He also held massive public meetings, calling for an electoral coalition of the left. The largest of these took place outside Madrid in October 1935, and was the largest political meeting in Spanish history. Perhaps as many as 500,000 people turned up to hear **Azaña** urge the masses to unite in defence of Spanish democracy against what many saw as the looming threat of fascism. He declared that 'All Europe today is a battlefield... between democracy, with all its shortcomings, with all its faults, with all its mistakes or errors, and tyranny with all its horrors... There is no choice. Ours is made.'

Largo Caballero was initially unwilling to go along with Azaña's ideas, but was finally persuaded by the changing attitude of Spain's small Communist Party. Taking their lead from Moscow, the Communists had toed the Stalinist line of non-co-operation with other parties, but this policy changed dramatically in 1935. Citing the growing threat of fascism throughout Europe, Moscow announced that national communist parties should work with others in forging anti-fascist alliances wherever necessary. As a result, in Spain the Socialist Party, along with the Communists, joined Azaña's coalition of parties to form the Popular Front in January 1936.

Azaña delivers his speech, October 1935

Azaña's speech

"All Europe today is a battlefield between democracy and its enemies, and Spain is not an exception. You must choose between democracy, with all its shortcomings, with all its faults, with all its mistakes or errors, and tyranny with all its horrors… In Spain one hears frivolous and vain talk of dictatorship. We find it repugnant not only by doctrine, but by experience and through good sense… Dictatorship is a consequence or political manifestation of intolerance; its propellant is fanaticism; and its means of action, physical violence. Dictatorship leads to war… it stupefies peoples and drives them mad."

Take note

Re-read the extract from Azaña's speech above. How accurately do you think his comments reflect the state of Spanish politics at the time?

Fascist links

Italy's fascist dictator, Benito Mussolini, was described as the **'Duce'**, or leader, from the early 1920s. Adolf Hitler of Germany took the same title, in German (*the Führer*), in 1934.

The end of the *Bienio Negro*, 1935

The suppression of the risings in Catalonia and Asturias led to growing support for the CEDA throughout 1935. The party began to adopt some of the trappings of fascism, including uniforms and badges, which had been adopted in Italy and Germany. In deliberate imitation of the **Duce** and the **Führer**, Gil Robles was hailed at public meetings as the *Jefe*, or the Chief. His speeches developed a tone which was increasingly anti-democratic and anti-republican. He made clear, not only his admiration for European fascism, but also his deep hatred of left-wing parties, trade unions and their members.

In May 1935 Gil Robles finally joined the government as Minister of War. He shared with most army officers a firm conviction that the army's most important duty was to preserve and protect traditional Spain from its enemies. To this end he appointed General Francisco Franco as Chief of the General Staff, and the two men worked together replacing liberal and republican officers with hardline traditionalists.

At the end of 1935, a bizarre gambling scandal, coupled with growing charges of ministerial corruption, persuaded Alcalá Zamora to dismiss the government. Gil Robles was convinced that he would be appointed Prime Minister, but he was to be bitterly disappointed when the President appointed a caretaker government and called fresh elections for February 1936.

Results of the *Bienio Negro*

None of the major political parties emerged from the *Bienio Negro* with any credit.

- The CEDA had been formed to promote and protect the interests of conservative Spain. By 1936, however, the CEDA leader, Gil Robles, was moving beyond this position. He was seriously contemplating the end of the Second Republic and the creation of some form of dictatorship.

- The Radical Republicans governed throughout the *Bienio Negro*. The party, and their leader Lerroux, were regarded by most Spaniards as a group of cynical opportunists without any political principles. It came as no surprise that its members were involved in corruption scandals at the end of 1935. Few Spaniards felt inclined to vote for the party in February 1936.

- The Socialists probably made more mistakes than any other party, and their errors were to be held against them in 1936 and beyond. They betrayed their supporters by refusing to join electoral coalitions in 1933, a decision which reduced them to an insignificant rump in the new Cortes. Largo Caballero's determination to pursue revolutionary policies rather than working within the Republic's constitution was largely responsible for the disastrous risings in Catalonia and Asturias in 1934. These errors were largely corrected by the decision to join the Popular Front in 1936, but by then it was perhaps too late to prevent the drift towards civil conflict.

Conclusion: How black was the *Bienio Negro*?

Despite all its failures and shortcomings, Azaña's government of 1931–33 had brought substantial benefits to most Spaniards, especially the peasants in the countryside. However, the only people to benefit from the *Bienio Negro* were those classes and groups which still stood for 'Old Spain'. The repeal of most of Azaña's anti-clerical laws helped the Catholic Church to recover some of its power and influence. The abolition of a number of rights for industrial workers and peasants was carried out solely for the benefit of the wealthy. In the years 1934–35 the CEDA had fulfilled the chief aims of its supporters. The majority of Spaniards, those who had greeted *La Niná Bonita* with such enthusiasm in 1931, felt disillusioned and betrayed. An ominous development was the growing feeling within the left that real change in Spain could only be achieved through violence and not through voting; the bullet was increasingly preferred to the ballot. Spain in 1936 had become a dangerously divided country.

Taking it further

You can read further reports on the Asturias rising in Anthony Beevor, *The Battle for Spain* (2007) and Paul Preston, *The Spanish Civil War* (2006).

Activity: Two rebellions

Compare the risings in Asturias in October 1934 and the Casas Viejas rebellion of January 1933 (Chapter 2). What are the similarities and the differences between the two rebellions? Think about the causes, events, suppression and effects of each revolt.

Activity: Reactions to the right

In Chapter 1, you made a list of key groups within Spanish society and wrote diary entries of their reactions to the king's departure.

- Revisit your list and write a short radio broadcast for a foreign (non–Spanish) audience for each group, identifying your reaction to and experiences of the *Bienio Negro*.

- How black were the 'Two Black Years' for each group?

Activity: Choosing sides

Imagine you are assigning a representative from each group within Spanish society to two teams in a five-aside football match. You will also need some 'fence-sitters' to referee the match.

- Decide on five figures to play for the 'Republican Reformers'. Number them in order of dedication to the cause.

- Decide on five figures to play for the 'Changeless Conservatives'. Number them in order of dedication to the cause.

- How easy is it to divide them into two 'camps', and are there any 'fence-sitters'?

Write a short report on how you would go about reconciling the two sides.

Skills Builder 1: **Planning answers to questions on causation and change**

Questions on causation

In the AS examination you may be asked questions on causation – questions about what caused historical events to take place.

Some questions may ask you to explain why something happened. For example:

> (A) Why did Azaña's government lose the election of November 1933?

Other questions on causation will ask you to assess the importance of one cause of an event in relation to other causes. These often begin with 'How far' or 'To what extent'. Here is an example:

> (B) How far do you agree that Azaña's anti-clerical policies were the main reason for his government's defeat in the elections of November 1933?

Planning your answer

Before you write your essay you need to make a plan. In the exam you will have to do this very quickly! The first thing to do is to identify the key points you will make in your answer. Let's look at some examples.

When planning an answer to Question (A) you need to note down reasons why Azaña's government lost the 1933 elections. You can do this in the form of a list or a concept map.

When planning an answer to Question (B) you need to think about the importance of each reason. You could:

- write a list of all the reasons then number them in order of importance
- draw a concept map with 'the government's defeat in November 1933' at the centre, and put the most important reasons near the middle and the least important reasons further away.

It is much easier to assess the importance of one factor when you have a list of all the relevant factors in front of you.

The information you require for these answers can be found in Chapters 2 and 3. Go to Chapters 2 and 3 and identify the reasons why the government was defeated.

Linking the causes

Once you have identified the relevant information and organised it, it is important to highlight links between the reasons.

In making your plan, try grouping together reasons which have links. If you have produced a list of reasons, you may want to rearrange the points where you can identify clear links between them. If you have drawn a concept map, you could draw arrows between the linked points.

Writing your answer

For Question (A) above, you could write a paragraph on each cause. Alternatively, you might want to start with what you think is the most important cause and then deal with the other causes.

For Question (B) above, it is essential that you refer to the relative importance of different causes, focusing particularly on the government's anti-clerical policies. Remember to answer the question! You might want to deal with anti-clericalism first and then assess the importance of other points explaining the government's defeat. Make sure you write a separate paragraph for each reason that you identify.

Questions about change

These questions will require you to explain how far a specified factor changed during a historical period.

Examples of this type of question would be:

> (C) How far did Azaña's government change Spanish society in the years 1931–33?

> (D) How far did divisions within Spanish society increase in the years 1931–33?

Planning your answer

When you plan, organise your material in a way that will help you to answer the question.

For instance, for Question (C) you could begin by listing two or three ways in which Spanish society changed. Having done that, you could list two or three ways in which change was limited. Alternatively, you could arrange this information on one or two concept maps. Remember that your answer needs to be balanced. Therefore, it should provide points for and against change.

Each of these points will form the basis for one paragraph in your answer. In the next Skills Builder section, you will consider the importance of providing specific examples to support your points. Don't forget to do this!

When you plan, there is no need to organise your material in a chronological way. This may encourage the writing of descriptive or narrative-style answers. Such answers may contain lots of accurate and relevant historical information, but may not be directly focused on the question.

Writing your answer

In Questions (C) and (D) you are asked 'how far' in relation to changes. So in your final paragraph, the conclusion, you will be expected to make a judgment. Based on the historical evidence you have presented in your answer, you should decide, and state, whether you believe the situation mainly changed or stayed the same.

Activity: How much have you learned?

Here are some examples of questions which deal with causation and change. First, identify the causation questions and give a reason to support your choice. Then identify the questions which deal with change and give a reason for your choice. Finally, choose one 'causation' question and one 'change' question and produce a plan for each, showing how you would organise your answer.

> (A) How far were the government's agrarian policies the main reason for its defeat in the elections of November 1933?

> (B) How accurate is it to say that the government of 1934–36 destroyed all the achievements of Azaña's government of 1931–33?

> (C) In what ways did opposition towards Azaña's government change in the years 1931–33?

Chapter 4: **The eve of war**

Key questions

- What was the impact of the election of February 1936 on the stability of the Spanish state?
- Why was the Republican government of 1936 weak?
- Why did General Mola launch a military coup in July 1936?

The creation of the Popular Front brought success for the left in the subsequent elections of February 1936. Following their victory, General Mola hatched a plan to overthrow the government and restore the right to power. Unintentionally, his actions sparked a civil war – however, he did not live to see its end. Mola was a superstitious man. Years beforehand a fortune-teller had foretold that he would die with his boots on. From that point on, fearing death in a plane crash, he always flew without his boots. Sadly for Mola, the fortune-teller was wrong. He was killed in a plane crash in 1937, without his boots.

Take note

1. Use the information in this chapter to produce two lists:
   - Groups/individuals who supported the Popular Front government.
   - Groups/individuals who did not support the Popular Front government.

These lists will be a useful point of reference as you study later events. Therefore, don't just record the names of the political parties – also, where possible, note down their beliefs and key policies (you may need to re-read information in previous chapters in order to do this).

2. Now use the information in this chapter to make a list of causes of the July 1936 coup.

Timeline

1936	16 February	General election in Spain: Popular Front coalition gained the most seats and Manuel Azaña became Prime Minister
	14 March	Falange banned
	25 March	Peasant occupation of farm land in Extremadura
	10 May	Azaña became President
	July	Falange membership reached 40,000
	12–13 July	José Castillo assassinated; José Calvo Sotelo assassinated General Mola issued secret message ordering a coup

The 1936 election

After two years of reactionary government, the February election of 1936 passed power back to the left. The right had won in 1933 by forming an electoral alliance (see page 21), which then created the basis of the ruling coalition. In the run-up to the 1936 election, the left did the same. Communists, liberals and socialists joined together to form the **Popular Front**. Alone on the left, the anarchists refused to join the coalition. They wanted to end government once and for all and therefore took no part in the election.

CEDA, however, would not give up without a fight, and tried a variety of tactics to hold on to power. Due to the right's dirty tricks, 20 Spanish villages registered no votes whatsoever for the Popular Front. Additionally, in some villages, such as Chite in the south of Spain, well-known Socialist politicians were jailed to stop them campaigning.

In spite of these efforts, the Popular Front won a healthy majority of seats in the Cortes and Manuel Azaña became Prime Minister of the new government. Nonetheless, this was not a convincing victory.

The Popular Front gained only 48% of the vote compared to the right's 46%, with around 1.5% of the electorate voting for the **Basque Nationalist Party**. These results demonstrated that there was no consensus about the future of Spain.

The Popular Front in power

Azaña's government alarmed the right. While there were no **Marxists** in the government, and most of the high-ranking ministers were middle-class liberals, the new government started undoing the changes that had been made during the *Bienio Negro*. First, it announced an immediate amnesty for all prisoners from the 1934 rising. Land reform restarted, and the government gave Catalonia political and administrative autonomy. Worse still, as far as the right were concerned, Largo Caballero called openly for a **Bolshevik**-style revolution. More worrying news for the right came in April, when the new government removed President Alcalá Zamora, replacing him with the less conservative Prime Minister Azaña. Some on the right saw this as the first step towards a Marxist revolution.

Popular Front election posters, February 1936

The situation in the Cortes was tense. Indeed, a speech by **José Calvo Sotelo**, the new leader of the right, led to a scuffle as one Socialist deputy called him a 'pimp' and offered to fight him in the street! However, the right were also concerned about events outside the capital. Growing violence allowed them to argue that the new government had lost control and that the country was sliding into chaos.

- In rural areas, poor peasants, impatient for land reform, seized land from the aristocracy. On 25 March, the first day of this movement, 60,000 peasants in the region of Extremadura took over 3000 farms. To the horror of many conservatives, Azaña's government did nothing to stop this. Rather, the Popular Front legalised the peasants' actions.

- In the cities, the UGT and CNT unions organised widespread strikes in protest against low wages. These often turned violent as union members were confronted by **Falange** militia.

- The Falange also attacked the right-wing CEDA, who they perceived as being too moderate. In response, the government banned the Falange and imprisoned their leader, but this did nothing to quell the unrest. Indeed, it led to a huge surge in support: by July, Falange membership had increased to 40,000.

Glossary

Popular Front

A coalition of left-wing and liberal political parties opposed to fascism, including the Socialists, the Communists, the Republican Left and the Republican Union Party, formed in reaction to the dominance of the right (the CEDA) in January 1936.

Basque Nationalist Party

People from the Basque region of northern Spain who fought for independence. The Basque people have a strong identity rooted in their own history, culture, tradition and language, and consequently, do not see themselves as part of Spain.

Marxism

A variety of socialism associated with Karl Marx (1818–1883), which asserts that in industrial societies the working class, increasingly poverty-stricken and desperate, will inevitably rise up and overthrow the ruling class by revolution.

Bolshevik

A revolutionary socialist political party who, in Russia in 1917, brought about the first successful communist seizure of power.

Glossary

Falange

Fascist party founded by José Antonio Primo de Rivera, son of the former dictator, in 1933. The Falange arguably bore prime responsibility for the increasing violence following the 1936 election.

The Falange, like all fascists, wanted to end class war by urging workers and employers to sacrifice their own interests to serve the nation. They did not believe in equality, but thought that all people could be united by nationalism. They also believed that most people were irrational, and therefore stressed the importance of propaganda and national myths rather than intellectual argument.

Carlists

A political group which wanted to restore the monarchy to Spain. In contrast to the Alphonsine Monarchists, they rejected the traditional monarchy in favour of another family line. The dispute can be dated back to 1830, when Ferdinand VII reintroduced mixed succession, giving women an equal right to inherit the throne of Spain. This change meant that Ferdinand's daughter inherited the throne, rather than his brother, Carlos. Carlists believed that the change was illegitimate and therefore Carlos' descendants were the rightful rulers of Spain. They also wholly rejected liberalism.

Coup

A military seizure of power.

Biography

José Calvo Sotelo

1893–1936

A leading Monarchist politician, Calvo Sotelo served as Primo de Rivera's finance minister and was forced into exile upon the dictator's fall. He returned to Spain in 1934, having been granted amnesty by the government, and became the leader of Spain's official opposition in the Cortes. He was assassinated by the left in retaliation for the murder of José Castillo in 1936.

The CEDA leader, Gil Robles, spoke out against the disorder in the Cortes. He claimed that the four months of Azaña's government had seen 269 murders, 300 large-scale strikes, and the destruction of 251 church buildings. His figures were exaggerated, but they gave an indication of the situation facing the country between February and July – a period sometimes called the 'little civil war'. Furthermore, they provided a pretext for action. Gil Robles had been arguing for a military uprising for some time, and the chaotic atmosphere provided the necessary excuse: the army would rebel against the government in order to restore order.

Mola's plan

Although Gil Robles played an important role in planning the plot against the government, the rebellion itself was initiated by **General Emilio Mola**. Mola wanted the army to turn against the government and take control of the country. From the start, he assumed that his plan would be successful. First, he thought that the army itself would be able to put down any resistance. Second, Mola knew that he had significant political backing. He could count on the support of a variety of right-wing groups and leading members of CEDA. What is more, he had even been able to engineer an alliance with the traditionalist **Carlists** and the radical Falange. The backing of political groups was important to Mola's plan as they would help to give the impression that the uprising had popular support. Additionally, groups like the Carlists and the Falange had militias which could support the **coup** if street fighting broke out.

Two assassinations

Mola had decided to act, but was uncertain about the timing of the coup. However, two assassinations in Madrid provided him with the justification he needed to launch his coup.

Biography

General Emilio Mola

1887–1937

A senior army general and Military Commander of Pamplona, a major city in Northern Spain, Mola is primarily remembered for his role instigating the coup against the government in 1936. He was intelligent and good natured, popular with the men under his command. He was killed in a plane crash in 1937– as General Sanjurjo had been the year before – leading to rumours that General Franco had ordered the assassination of his rivals.

The first assassination came on 12 July. José Castillo, a well-known left-wing member of the Assault Guard, was murdered as he left for work. On learning of his death, his colleagues decided to retaliate, drawing up a death list of prominent right-wing targets. After failing to find Gil Robles, the Assault Guard arrested the Monarchist leader José Calvo Sotelo and later killed him. He anticipated his murder, telling his wife that he would call her soon, 'unless these gentlemen blow my brains out'. Sotelo's murder had not been ordered by the government, but there was no way that they could escape blame for the actions of their own police force. Conservatives were outraged, and Mola made up his mind. Within hours of the assassination, secret messages were dispatched ordering the coup.

Conclusion: Why did the Second Republic come to an end?

The Second Republic had been torn apart by political disagreements. Following the 1936 election, it was clear that democracy had failed to solve the tensions at the heart of Spanish society. Left and right both turned to violence. Republican death squads took to the streets as Mola seized the opportunity to launch a military takeover.

Activity: Who was responsible for the coup?

You will need the notes you made as you read this chapter.

In the middle of a large piece of paper, copy the list of causes of the July 1936 coup.

- On the left-hand side, copy the list of groups or individuals who supported the Popular Front government.

- On the right-hand side, copy the list of groups or individuals who did not support the Popular Front government.

- Draw lines between the list in the centre of the page and the lists to either side. These lines should link causes of the coup to the people or groups responsible for these events.

- Write brief notes above your lines to explain the links.

Use your diagram to write a paragraph in answer to the question 'How far did the Popular Front government bring the coup upon itself?'

Activity: Signs of trouble

In the next chapter, you will read about events during the coup. You will discover that the coup failed to overthrow the Republican government, but that the Republican government failed to conquer the coup.

What evidence is there in this chapter – and previous chapters – that:

- the right-wing coup would fail?

- the Republican government would not be strong enough to reassert control?

Take note

As you read through these sections, answer the questions below:
1. Why did General Mola want to launch a coup?
2. Why did Mola assume that his coup would be successful?
3. In what ways did the assassinations of July 1936 provide Mola with an opportunity to launch his coup?

Taking it further

Helen Graham's book *The Spanish Civil War: a Very Short Introduction* (2005) provides a clear and concise summary of the events that led to the outbreak of war. Locate a copy of the book and read Chapter 1. Use it to supplement your notes on this period. In addition, you could consult *The Spanish Civil War* by Paul Preston (2006).

Chapter 5: **The fighting begins**

Key questions
- How successful was General Mola's coup?
- Who supported the coup?
- How far was the coup the major cause of the Spanish Civil War?

The Republican government knew that Francisco Franco, formerly the Chief of the General Staff, was a potential danger. With this in mind, they had posted him to the Canary Islands, believing that there he would be out of harm's way. However, the government had not counted on British flying ace Captain Cecil Bebb. Bebb was approached by Franco's press officer and asked to take Franco to Morocco to participate in the coup. A Spanish plane landing on the islands would have alerted the authorities, but a British plane would attract little attention. Bebb agreed to the plan. He later explained that, on being asked to fly to the Canary Islands to pick up a general who was going to join a rebellion against the Spanish state, he thought 'what a delightful idea, what a great adventure'.

Take note

As you read through this section, make three lists:
- Reasons why Mola chose Franco to lead the coup.
- Ways in which the coup was a failure.
- Ways in which the coup was a success.

The armies of Spain

The Spanish Army consisted of two separate forces:
- the Peninsular Army – over 100,000 men – based in mainland Spain
- the Army of Africa – 34,000 men – the army's elite troops, based in Morocco.

The military coup

The coup was launched on 17 July in Spanish North Morocco. Francisco Franco, who arrived in Morocco a day later, played an important role. Mola had chosen Franco to lead the Army of Africa, the **Spanish army**'s elite force, during the rebellion. Franco was an obvious choice. He enjoyed a great deal of respect among the Army of Africa. Moreover, Franco had proved to be a gifted general. At the age of 22, he had become the youngest captain in the Spanish army. He had fought bravely in 1916 in El Biutz, where he was wounded, allegedly losing a testicle. Ten years later he became the army's youngest general. Mola also chose Franco because he had proven himself to be an enemy of the radicals. Indeed, in 1934 he had headed the Army of Africa division that had put down the Asturias rising.

On July 18 the coup spread to the mainland. However, Mola's plan failed to overthrow the government in one swift stroke. Indeed, in five of Spain's seven largest cities the army was defeated by the local militia fighting alongside the police and troops loyal to the government. Most importantly, local army leaders were defeated in Madrid as General Rafael Villegas, who was supposed to be leading the rebellion, went into hiding. Eventually, General Fanjul took control, locking himself and 2500 troops in the Montana barracks. This was a disastrous move. Within 24 hours the base had been overrun by the Republican militia and the soldiers massacred.

There were, however, military successes. General Queipode de Llano swiftly took control of Seville in the south, General Mola, backed by the Carlist militia, took Pamplona, and much of Western Andalusia fell to the rebels. Significantly, the military had succeeded in weakening the Republic.

The government relied on the army and the police force to control its territory, but the majority of the army and a significant proportion of the police had gone over to the rebels. Consequently, immediately after the coup, the government had little control of Spain.

The division of Spain

Franco and Mola, August 1936

> ### Take note
>
> A wide range of people and political groups were involved in the Spanish Civil War, and it can be difficult to remember who supported which side, and why they did this.
>
> The following section describes how the Spanish population was divided. As you read through this section, complete the unshaded parts of the table below. A section in the next chapter will explain which political groups supported each side. Chapter 7 will describe the international support given to the Republicans and the Nationalists. Title the table 'Who supported who in the Spanish Civil War?' and keep it at the front of your files so that you can refer to it as you work through the course.

		Who?	Why?
Republicans	Public support		
	Political support		
	International support		
Nationalists	Public support		
	Political support		
	International support		

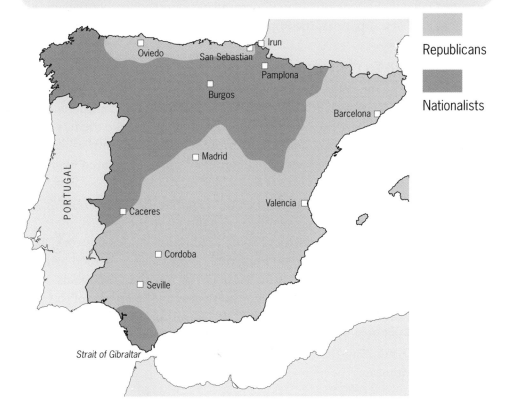

Republicans

Nationalists

The division of Spain, July 1936

In the aftermath of the failed coup, Spain was divided between Nationalists – who supported the army rebellion – and Republicans – who sided with the government, or at least opposed the army. In part, the division of Spain reflected the country's history, and social and regional divisions.

The army rebels tended to succeeded in areas where monarchism – of one sort or another – was strong. In Pamplona, for example, the Carlist militia, the Falangists and the police marched in support of the rebellion, easily crushing those who remained loyal to the government. In addition, the army rebels did well in most of north-west Spain, where church goers were hostile to the 'Godless' Republic. In these areas, devout Catholic peasants and workers also tended to back the rebels. Former CEDA voters, including almost all of the aristocracy and the vast majority of the middle class, also supported the Nationalists. Finally, almost two-thirds of the army's junior officers rebelled.

Urban areas tended to be Republican strongholds, as the workers supported the government's progressive labour reforms. This support was crucial as the unions quickly organised the workers to resist the army's rebellion. Similarly, most poor peasants backed the government as they feared that the Nationalists would reverse land reform. Religion also played a part. In areas where anti-clericalism was strong, such as Catalonia, the people supported the Republicans.

However, Spain was a deeply divided society, with Republicans also found in largely conservative areas and Nationalists also present in government strongholds. This led to widespread bloodshed as both sides tried to root out opposition in the areas that they controlled. In mainland Spain, the trained military and police forces were split. Furthermore, despite Mola's plan to use the army to overthrow the government, 17 of the army's top 21 generals remained loyal to the Republic. Equally surprising was the fact that the air force and the navy supported the Republicans.

From the coup to civil war

Immediately after the coup, the situation looked bleak for the rebels. Things were so bad that Mola initially thought his best option was to commit suicide. Having failed to take Madrid, Mola marched south to try to take the city himself. However, a shortage of arms, determined resistance from local militias and police, and the Guadarrama mountain range prevented his forces from reaching the capital.

The initial advantage appeared to lie with the Republicans. The people of Madrid remained loyal to the government and therefore the government were able to quickly restore control of Spain's communications network, as well as the gold reserves. The urban industrial centres also remained loyal, ensuring that they could produce arms more effectively than the rebels. Furthermore, the government was able to capitalise on the loyalty of the navy and organise a blockade of the **Strait of Gibraltar** which left the Army of Africa stranded in North Africa. The rebels had succeeded in capturing almost half of Spain. But their greatest advantage – the elite Army of Africa – was stuck in Morocco.

Glossary

Strait of Gibraltar

The stretch of water separating Spain from Morocco and joining the Atlantic Ocean to the Mediterranean Sea.

Yet the Republic failed to make the most of its advantages, and adopted a defensive strategy. The rebels, by contrast, were quickly on the offensive again. Significantly, army rebels benefited from foreign aid. Franco was well connected. He approached two German businessmen who were based in Morocco, asking them to take a letter requesting assistance to **Hitler**. Soon, Rudolf Hess, Hitler's deputy, sent a private plane to pick them up and they were able to present Franco's request directly to the *Führer*. The German leader decided to help immediately and sent 20 Junker 52 transport planes to Morocco, placing them under Franco's direct control. The planes arrived on 28 July and immediately began airlifting the Army of Africa to join General de Llano's forces in Seville. In the last days of July, 1500 troops were airlifted to mainland Spain, and the pace continued with 500 troops being airlifted every day from early August. The Italian dictator **Mussolini** also sent bomber planes to cover merchant ships ferrying troops across the Strait of Gibraltar. It was these interventions that allowed the army rebels to keep fighting and turned the failed coup into a civil war.

The causes of the Spanish Civil War

The coup was the trigger for civil war in Spain, but it was not the sole cause. Long-term factors such as social and political tensions, the weakness of Spain's commitment to democracy, regional differences and the loss of the Spanish Empire undermined the Republic. In addition, short-term economic problems, the international situation, class divisions and the weakness of political moderates contributed to the outbreak of war. In short, the Second Republic was consumed by civil war because it was rejected by increasing numbers who were prepared to fight for alternatives on both the left and the right.

Long-term causes

- There were serious tensions between the great landowners of the south – the *latifundistas* – and the day labourers who worked their farms for a pittance. The day labourers resented poor working conditions and terrible pay. In turn, the landowners were afraid of the day labourers and saw them as a potentially revolutionary force.

- In the industrialised cities of the north, industrialisation and poor working conditions led to the development of radical ideas among the working class. As a result, the middle class – who were numerically small and politically weak – feared that democracy would lead to radical socialism.

- Before the Second Republic, political power was largely in the hands of those who did not support democracy: the landowners, the Church and the monarchy. These groups saw trade union rights, redistribution of land to the peasants and religious and political freedom as a threat to their position of power.

- Many people in Catalonia and the Basque Country wanted greater autonomy or total independence from Spain. As these regions were among the most industrialised in the country, this was seen as a significant threat by those who wanted Spain to remain as it was.

Biography

Adolf Hitler

1889–1945

Leader of the Nazi Party, a fascist political organisation, and *Führer* (sole leader) of Germany from 1933–45. In the opening months of the war, 10,500 men were flown across the Strait of Gibraltar by the German *Luftwaffe* (air force), allowing the Nationalists the chance to fight on. German assistance was co-ordinated by Lieutenant Colonel Warlimont of the German General Staff, military adviser to General Franco.

Biography

Benito Mussolini

1883–1945

Leader of the Italian Fascist Party, and *Duce* (sole leader) of Italy from 1922–43, Mussolini was the first fascist dictator and influenced both Hitler's and Franco's ideas. In December 1936, Mussolini began to supply the Nationalists with men and equipment.

Glossary

May Day

May Day is traditionally a day on which workers celebrate their contribution to society and campaign for greater rights. For this reason, it is sometimes known as Labour Day, or even International Workers' Day. In Spain in 1936, the workers celebrated as usual, but on this occasion they held up banners depicting Largo Caballero, chanted his name and called for him to instigate a revolution.

Short-term causes

Spain was considerably poorer after five years of the Second Republic and economic problems further destabilised the government. Spain's economic problems were part of the global depression, which affected countries across the world, but the Republic took the blame. Many Spaniards turned to radicals on either the left or the right for a solution.

The international political situation also weakened the authority of the Republic. In America, Britain and France, democracy appeared to be in trouble as democratic politics struggled to solve the problems of the Great Depression. Countries that had rejected democracy appeared to be doing much better. For example, the economy of Stalin's Russia was growing at a rate of 13% a year. Similarly, there was much talk of a Nazi 'economic miracle' in Germany, where unemployment halved in the first two years of Hitler's government and continued to decline. We now know that these economic 'achievements' were not nearly as impressive as they seemed but, in the 1930s, radical anti-democratic regimes appeared to be succeeding where democratic nations failed.

The traditional battle between reactionaries and reformers continued during the Second Republic. The battle was still fought along class lines, with the workers and the peasants supporting the reforms that the aristocracy and many of the middle class opposed. On the right, traditional Catholics feared that Spain was abandoning God's ways, landowners wanted to end land reform once and for all, business leaders felt threatened by the power of the unions and the army feared further national betrayal by weak and treacherous politicians. For a time, the right were prepared to work within the rules of the Republic. But, for many on the right, the election of 1936 showed that democracy could not be trusted to save Spain. On the left, the growing influence of communists and anarchists further weakened the Republic. The anarchists wanted to destroy all government, and the Republic was no exception. The communists wanted to destroy the capitalist Republic and replace it with a workers' state.

On both sides, the influence of moderates withered and the strength of the radicals grew. On the left, the 1936 **May Day** demonstrations in Madrid showed the popularity of revolutionaries such as Largo Caballero. Similarly, on the right, CEDA's Gil Robles, who was formerly considered to be an extreme conservative, was eclipsed by the monarchist Calvo Sotelo, whose radical conservatism surpassed that of the CEDA right. Even elements in the aristocracy began to radicalise, as large numbers of young aristocrats joined the Falange. As politics polarised, compromise became impossible and conflict appeared inevitable.

Conclusion: Why did civil war break out in Spain in 1936?

Mola's coup was the spark that ignited the Spanish Civil War, but the causes were long-standing. Spanish society was riddled with deep-rooted social differences. Reforms which helped the poor threatened the established power of the rich. Democracy had failed to reach a compromise between the competing demands of the powerful and the powerless. Spain was also split along regional lines, a fact that distressed Spanish nationalists who wanted a unified nation under a strong central government. Furthermore, Spanish culture was coping with the loss of empire. Radicals in the army and the Falange believed that democracy was incapable of restoring Spain's glory and therefore looked to the example of Hitler and Mussolini, who had established fascist regimes to recover their nation's honour. Radicals on the left also believed that democracy had failed. However, they wanted to replace it with either communism or anarchism. In this context, it is no surprise that Mola's coup precipitated a bitter civil war.

Activity: This house believes...

In the book *History in Dispute – The Spanish Civil War* (2004), the historians Nigel Townson and Julius Ruiz discuss to what extent the outbreak of the Spanish Civil War was inevitable. Townson argues that 'none of the political or economic crises experienced immediately before 1936 made the war inevitable'. On the opposing side, Ruiz claims that tensions between those who supported democracy and those who opposed it were so great that war could not have been prevented. Your task is to debate this issue formally.

- Divide into two teams. The first team must defend the motion that the outbreak of the Spanish Civil War was inevitable. The second must oppose this.

- Find points and examples. If you are defending the motion, consider the evidence that suggests that Spanish democracy was fundamentally unstable. If you are opposing the motion, find evidence to show that there were points at which civil war could have been averted.

- Each team should appoint a team leader who should prepare a five-minute speech outlining the team's argument.

- An impartial Chair should also be appointed to oversee the debate and award points, and to ensure politeness and fair play is maintained.

- Each leader should present their team's speech, proposing or opposing the motion.

- Following the speeches, the floor is opened for contributions (in the form of questions or comments) from the other members of the team. Points are awarded by the Chair using the following system:
  1 point for each relevant question.   2 points for each general statement.
  5 points for each general statement supported by a specific example.

- At the end of the debate, the team with the most points wins.

Taking it further

Use a programme such as Microsoft Movie Maker to create a short film about the causes of the Spanish Civil War. Search the internet for images that illustrate the different groups and different tensions that led to the conflict. Import these into the movie-making software and provide a commentary, explaining a) the ways in which the different groups and tensions undermined Spanish democracy, and b) how the images relate to the factors you are describing.

Skills Builder 2: **Writing in paragraphs**

In the examination you will have to write an essay-style answer on this topic, in approximately 40 minutes. When producing an essay-style answer, it is important that you write in paragraphs. You will need to make a number of points to build up your argument so that it answers the question you have been asked. You should write a paragraph to address each point.

What should you include in a paragraph?

In a paragraph you should:

- Make a point to support your argument and answer the question.
- Provide evidence to support your point.
- Explain how your evidence supports your point.
- Explain how your points relate to the essay question.

Remember: POINT — EVIDENCE — EXPLANATION

It is important that you construct your answer this way. If you just 'tell a story' in which you produce factual knowledge without explanation in relation to the question, you will not get high marks.

An example

Here is an example of a question asking you to produce not a story, but an explanation:

> (A) Why did civil war break out in Spain in 1936?

The information to answer this question can be found in Sections 1 and 2. The reasons you could include are:

- long-term factors: lack of a democratic culture in Spain, need for economic reform, and social divisions within Spain
- political factors: the failure of the Second Republic
- short-term factors: assassinations and growing violence
- trigger: Mola's coup.

As you plan, it is important to have a clear idea about the significance of these reasons. To do this, you must decide which factor was the most important. Your answer should convince the examiner that your opinion is correct.

Here is an example of a paragraph which could form part of your answer:

The most important reason why civil war broke out in Spain in 1936 was the coup launched on 17 July 1936. The coup was organised by General Mola, a senior general, based in Pamplona. As soon as the coup spread from Morocco to the Spanish mainland, Spanish society divided into two opposing camps: Nationalists, who supported the coup, and Republicans, who supported the existing government. The Nationalists enjoyed the support of most former CEDA voters, the aristocracy, the vast majority of the middle class, the bulk of the Catholic Church and the middle ranks of the army. By contrast, the Republicans gained the support of most workers and peasants, and nationalists in the Spanish regions, such as the Basque Country and Catalonia. These divisions already existed in Spanish society, but the coup caused the civil war because the two sides armed themselves, triggering widespread fighting.

This is a good paragraph because:

- It begins with a clear statement which assesses a reason for the outbreak of civil war.
- It *prioritises* reasons by stating, in the opening sentence, that this was the key reason.
- The opening statement is backed up by evidence. It provides examples of the ways in which Mola's coup led to civil war.

Activity: Spot the mistake

Below are three paragraphs which attempt to explain why civil war broke out in Spain in 1936. However, although the information in each paragraph is correct, there are mistakes in the way each one is written. Your task is to spot the mistake in each paragraph and write one sentence of advice to the author of each paragraph explaining how they could do better.

Example 1

The Spanish Civil War broke out because of a coup launched in Spanish Morocco on 17 July 1936. The coup was organised by General Mola. However, General Francisco Franco, an army veteran who had been stationed in the Canary Islands by the Republican government in order to keep him out of trouble, was also involved. Franco was the leader of the Army of Africa, an elite fighting force and the best in the Spanish Army. The coup began in Morocco and spread to the mainland a day later, when General Mola and his forces attacked government forces in Pamplona. Similar action was taken throughout Spain.

Example 2

One reason why civil war broke out in Spain in 1936 was that a coup was launched. The coup was launched by the army and was intended to overthrow the government. People in Spain took sides after the coup: some supported it and some opposed it. This led to war.

Example 3

One reason why the civil war broke out in Spain was General Mola's coup. On 18 July 1936 Franco, under orders from General Mola, joined a rebellion against the Spanish government from Morocco. Rebel forces also fought the government in mainland Spain. Initially the government seemed to come out on top, but then with the aid of a German airlift, Franco's forces were taken to the mainland and were able to turn the coup into a full civil war. German help was extremely important and one of the main reasons why the Nationalists won the civil war.

Answers

Example 1 – this paragraph tells the story of the coup but does not answer the question.

Example 2 – this paragraph is focused on the question, but lacks specific detail.

Example 3 – this paragraph is generally well written, but the final sentence goes off the point of the question.

Activity: Write your own paragraph

Now try writing a paragraph on one of the other reasons for the outbreak of civil war. The information you require is found throughout Sections 1 and 2.

Remember to begin your paragraph by stating which factor you are going to address. Make sure that you support your answer with factual knowledge and evidence. Then conclude your paragraph by explaining how the evidence it provides answers the question.

Chapter 6: The military campaigns

Key questions

- How far were the Republicans divided in their ideology and military tactics?
- How far were the Nationalists united in their ideology and military tactics?
- What were the key phases of the Spanish Civil War?
- How did Franco's leadership help the Nationalists to win the Spanish Civil War?

Franco was celebrated in Nationalist propaganda as a military hero and tactical genius. However, Franco's military strategy was far from cutting-edge. Foreign observers thought that Franco was still using the tactics of the First World War – tactics almost two decades out of date. The new tactic, originating in Germany, was the *Blitzkrieg* – a war fought in the air and on the land simultaneously, at lightning speed. Nonetheless, Franco's old-school tactics were perfectly suited to the Spanish Civil War. By fighting a long and old-fashioned war, Franco played to the strengths of his army and exposed the weaknesses of his opponents.

Take note

As you read through the following section, complete the table below to show the key points of agreement and difference amongst the various factions within each side:

	Key points of agreement	Key differences
Republicans		
Nationalists		

Consider the information in your table. Based on this information alone, which side would you expect to be victorious in the Spanish Civil War? Write a paragraph explaining your answer.

Timeline

1936	27 September	Franco's forces captured Alcázar Castle in Toledo
	3 November	Franco's troops came within sight of Madrid
	23 November	Nationalist commanders called off assault on Madrid
1937	5–27 February	Battle of Jarama (to cut off supplies to Madrid)
	31 March	Mola's offensive in the North began
	26 April	Carpet bombing of Guernica
	19 June	Bilbao fell to the Nationalists
	6–24 July	Republican offensive at Brunete
	24 August	Republican offensive in Aragon launched
	26 August	Santander fell to the Nationalists
	6–22 September	Battle of El Mazuco – the fall of Asturias to the Nationalists
	15 December– 22 February 1938	Battle of Teruel – Republicans gained then lost the town; northern coast now entirely in Nationalist hands
1938	24 July–16 November	Battle of Ebro – Republican offensive to relieve Valencia
	23 December– 26 January 1939	Battle of Catalonia – Nationalist victory
1939	28 March	Madrid fell to the Nationalists
	1 April	Franco declared the end of the war

Unity and division – political support

Republicans

The Republican side was united in its opposition to the Nationalists, but divided over its hopes for the future of Spain. On the left wing were the anarchists. They wanted an immediate revolution which would destroy all government once and for all. Also on the left were the Marxists.

They too wanted a revolution, but one which would establish a workers' government. But, within this group, opinion was divided about the timing of the revolution. The Spanish Communist Party (the PCE), who took their orders from the USSR, believed that Spain was not yet ready for a revolution. Therefore, they fought to defend the Republic. The Trotskyite **POUM** led by **Andreu Nin**, wanted an immediate revolution to overthrow the Republic, followed by a revolutionary war against the Nationalists. The Spanish Socialist Party (the PSOE) was itself divided. The right wing of the PSOE supported the Republic, but wanted greater rights for workers, whereas some on the left argued for a revolution and were closer to POUM. Finally, there were middle-class liberals who, like the right-wing members of the PSOE, supported the Republic and rejected any kind of revolution.

Biography

Andreu Nin

1892–1937

A former secretary to Leon Trotsky, Nin was a member of the PCE before forming POUM (in 1935) in order to fight for an immediate workers' revolution. He was a government minister, but was sacked in December 1936 when the Soviets threatened to withdraw their aid. The PCE viewed him as a traitor, due to the fact that he was a Trotskyite, and demanded his arrest – along with the rest of the POUM leadership. He was tortured and murdered by the Communist secret police (SIM) in June 1937.

Factional fighting on the left meant that the Republicans were never able to rally around one leader. Francisco Largo Caballero of the PSOE became Prime Minister in September, with the hope of uniting the anti-Nationalist forces. However, the ideological divisions proved to be impossible to overcome and therefore, in a sense, the Republican government was fighting two civil wars, one against the Nationalists and the other against radicals in its own territory.

The Republicans were also split regarding the best way to defeat the Nationalists. Middle-class liberals, the PSOE and the Communists argued that a disciplined, centralised and traditional army was the only way to beat Franco. The anarchists and POUM believed that a traditional army was deeply undemocratic and a betrayal of their revolutionary principles. They favoured a highly decentralised and democratic people's militia.

In practice, both kinds of armies fought against the Nationalists, revealing weaknesses in both styles. The structure of the anarchist people's militia made them disorganised and slow to make decisions, while the strictness of communist centralisation made the traditional armies inflexible. These different approaches made it very hard for the forces fighting the Nationalists to co-operate.

Nationalists

Initially, the Nationalists were as deeply divided as the Republicans. Conservatives, many of whom had supported CEDA, wanted to restore order, stamp out the threat of communism, end the rule of corrupt politicians, ban trade unions and reassert the authority of the army and the Church.

Take note

As you read through this section, complete the 'Political support' sections of your 'Who supported who in the Spanish Civil War?' table. As you complete the section for the Republicans, remember to distinguish between those groups who wanted to defeat the Nationalists and re-establish the Republican government, and those that wanted to defeat the Nationalists and establish a different regime in Spain.

Glossary

POUM

There was considerable disagreement about how Marx's teachings applied to Spain, and therefore Marxists formed and joined different organisations, such as POUM, PCE and PSOE. The POUM was a Marxist political party, with its own militia, that believed the working class should immediately overthrow the Spanish government in a workers' revolution. The official Spanish Communist Party (PCE) described them as 'Trotskyite', alleging that they followed the teachings of Leon Trotsky, a Russian revolutionary who was viewed as a traitor by the Russian communist government.

Conversely, the Falange did not want to revive the old Spain, they wanted Spain to be reborn. They favoured a social revolution which would break the power of the aristocracy and the middle class. Finally, the Carlists and the monarchists wanted Spain to have a king again, although they disagreed on who the king should be.

Franco and the Nationalists

Franco played a crucial role in uniting the various factions and turning the Nationalists into a disciplined force capable of winning the war. Franco enjoyed widespread support because of his military prowess. Carlists, Falangists and people in all factions on the Nationalist side recognised this and supported him because of his heroism.

Franco also quickly asserted his authority in the army, which controlled the growing Nationalist zone. The army had planned to appoint the exiled General José Sanjurjo as their commander-in-chief, but he died in a plane crash on his way back to Spain. General Miguel Cabanellas took temporary command until, in September, a meeting of generals in Salamanca named Franco as the new ***Generalissimo***.

Franco was the obvious choice as leader for several reasons:

- He was the leader of the Army of Africa, the Spanish Army's elite corps.

- He was the only senior Nationalist leader who had successfully acquired aid from abroad.

- He was the most successful of the Nationalist generals. Following the airlift of the Army of Africa to mainland Spain, he was able to advance quickly, gaining a great deal of ground and scoring a string of military victories, quickly gaining respect from Nationalists for his successes.

- He was also a shrewd politician. He kept his political position unclear. Certainly, he was a conservative, but beyond this he was careful to make no political statement that would alienate any of the groups on the Nationalist side.

- Finally, he had luck on his side, as the Falange leader Primo de Rivera was in prison and therefore unable to dispute Franco's authority.

Following Primo de Rivera's execution by the Republicans in November 1936, Franco demonstrated his supreme political skill by merging the Carlist party and the Falange into a single movement – the *Movimiento Nacional* – with himself as the ***Caudillo*** or leader. In so doing, he ensured their loyalty and the unity of the Nationalists.

Glossary

Generalissimo

A title given to Franco, giving him supreme military authority during the civil war.

Caudillo

A leader with supreme political and military authority.

Franco's troops enter Malaga, August 1937

The civil war

The war comprised four broad phases:

- First, during July 1936–February 1937, the Nationalists tried (and failed) to capture Madrid.

- Second, in March 1937, they began to advance northwards towards Asturias, Santander and the Basque Country.

- Third, during July–December 1937, the Republicans mounted an unsuccessful counter-attack in the south.

- Finally, during 1938–39, the Nationalists advanced west, towards the Mediterranean, bringing about the fall of the Republic by the end of March 1939.

The Battle for Madrid, 1936–37

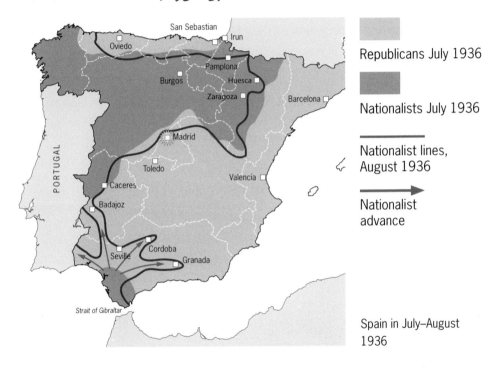

Republicans July 1936

Nationalists July 1936

Nationalist lines, August 1936

Nationalist advance

Spain in July–August 1936

Following the failed coup, the Nationalists turned their attention to Madrid, for whoever controlled the capital could claim authority over the whole of Spain. General Mola's troops advanced towards the city from Pamplona in the north, but shortages of manpower and supplies meant he was unable to take the city itself. Franco's troops advanced from the south. His army moved swiftly and it appeared that he would capture Madrid by the end of October.

However, Franco had other ideas. Rather than pressing on to Madrid, Franco ordered his troops to rescue the rebels who were under siege in the **Alcázar** (castle) in Toledo – whilst the Nationalist leaders debated appointing a sole commander. The Alcázar had no strategic value and the detour allowed the Republic more time to organise its defences, thereby jeopardising the capture of Madrid.

Take note

1. Copy the timeline at the beginning of this chapter. Colour-code the events on the timeline to show the four phases of the Spanish Civil War.
2. As you read through this chapter, write a 'headline' for each phase, summarising the key events and indicating which side emerged victorious.
3. Below each 'headline', list the reasons why the relevant side was able to emerge victorious. Remember that this list should include not only the strengths of the side that emerged victorious, but also the weaknesses of the side that was defeated.

Taking it further

Produce a 'Spanish civil war in two minutes' podcast. Think carefully about what to include. It is important that listeners are able to gain an overview of the events of the civil war and see their significance. However, also be creative: could you use sound effects rather than words to convey events quickly?

The seige of the Alcázar

Following the coup, Republican forces gained the upper hand in Toledo and Nationalists retreated to the Alcázar (castle). The Republicans surrounded the Alcázar on 21 July 1936. The Nationalists trapped in the castle endured the siege until late September and in so doing became a symbol of heroism for the Nationalist forces. Franco's first attempt to help them was to arrange for a plane to drop crates of food into the castle, along with a message stating that help was on its way. Franco's forces won a victory that symbolised the courage and endurance of the Nationalists by fighting off the Republican forces and 'liberating' their comrades.

From Paul Preston's biography of Franco

"Franco's absence from the campaign to take Madrid was quite remarkable. Perhaps he suspected that there was little easy glory to be won in Madrid and so slyly left Mola to take responsibility."
(*Franco*, Preston 1995)

Franco's actions revealed his true priorities. The soldiers at the Alcázar were Nationalist heroes and coming to their aid was a popular decision amongst the Nationalists. When, on 27 September, Franco's forces captured the castle, he won a great deal of support. Consequently, on 1 October, he was confirmed as Head of State, the undisputed leader of the Nationalists.

Nonetheless, Franco's delay had repercussions for the Nationalists. By the time Franco's forces reached Madrid, the Republic was in a much stronger position. As a result, the Nationalist offensives failed. Therefore, in mid-November, Franco ordered a change of tactics, abandoning direct assault in favour of a siege. Operations such as the Battle of Jarama in February 1937 aimed to cut off supply routes to the city. However, these efforts were unsuccessful. By spring 1937 it was clear that there would be no immediate victory for the Nationalists in Madrid.

There were several reasons for the Nationalists' failure:

- The Republicans captured the Nationalist army's battle plans, allowing them to counter their attack as they knew where to focus their forces.

- The morale of Madrid's citizens was high following the arrival of the International Brigades (see Chapter 7).

- The Republic could count on 23,000 soldiers compared to the Nationalists' 8000.

- The Republican militia was better suited to street fighting than Franco's traditionally trained forces.

- Until November, Franco left the attack on Madrid to Mola, rather than commanding the troops and devising the strategy himself.

- Mola's plans were unrealistic as they did not take account of the Republic's preparation for the attack.

Franco's leadership in the early part of the civil war was highly significant in the following ways:

- He was able to unite the various factions on the Nationalist side.

- His decision to march to Toledo rather than Madrid gave the Republicans a chance to organise themselves and therefore prolonged the civil war.

Nationalist victories in the north, 1937

The war in the north was a Nationalist offensive against the regions of Asturias, Santander and the Basque Country. The campaign began at the end of March 1937, under Mola's control. Mola's army attacked from the east, west and south, whilst the navy blockaded the north. Mola was aided by a German commander, Hugo Sperrle, head of the airborne **Condor Legion**.

Initially, Nationalist progress was slow. This was partly due to Franco, who favoured a World War I style **war of attrition** rather than a faster-moving more modern war. Franco was also keen to show that he, rather than Mola, was in control, and therefore transferred troops away from the war in the north to reinforce the siege of Madrid.

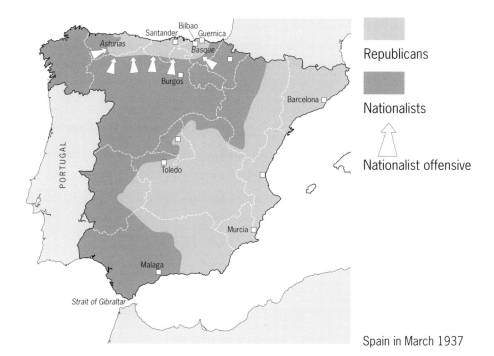

Republicans

Nationalists

Nationalist offensive

Spain in March 1937

The advance was also hindered by disagreements between Mola and Sperrle. Mola wanted to fight a swift war of annihilation, destroying whole towns, factories and farms. Sperrle advised moving more slowly in order to preserve the resources of the Basque Country. This would allow the Nationalists to use these resources once they had conquered the north.

From early April, the pace of the offensive quickened. Franco visited the northern front and settled the dispute between Mola and Sperrle. Unexpectedly, Franco backed Mola, allowing Mola's forces to conquer the Basque Country at the Battle of Bilbao in June. However, Mola – killed in a plane crash in that month – did not live to see the victory.

The Nationalist campaign in the Basque Country witnessed one of the worst military horrors of the war – the carpet bombing of Guernica. Wave after wave of the Condor Legion's *Behelfsbombers* dropped over 40 tonnes of bombs in three hours, while German fighter planes machine-gunned civilians who were trying to escape. Indeed, escape from the town was almost impossible as Italian *Sparviero* bombers had destroyed the bridges around the town. Guernica was completely flattened, and the Basque authorities claimed that the raid resulted in 1,654 dead and 889 wounded (though recent research suggests much lower figures). Significantly, the bombers targeted civilians rather than industry or army bases, in order to break the will of the population and force their surrender and to deter further resistance in the region.

Guernica: the aftermath of carpet bombing

During August, the province of Santander fell to the Nationalists, although much more slowly than many senior Nationalists had hoped. Following Mola's death, Franco reasserted his preference for a slow-paced war of attrition, thus delaying progress in the north. Asturias was the final northern province to fall, following the Battle of El Mazuco in September.

The Nationalists were successful in the north for the following reasons:

● They had control of the air. The German Condor Legion flew unopposed during the campaign. Republican planes, which were based in Madrid, did not have the range to fly to the northern territories.

● The Republic's northern outpost was cut off from the rest of its territory and therefore they had no direct support from the rest of the Republic.

● The Nationalist navy blockaded the northern shores, ensuring that no supplies could reach the north by sea.

● Political and cultural divisions between the three northern regions stood in the way of constructing a united defence.

Franco played an important role in the following ways:

● Franco's old-fashioned tactics and interference with Mola's plans slowed down the campaign in the north.

● However, in the long-run, the war of attrition exposed the weaknesses in the Republican army.

● Franco sorted out the differences between Mola and Sperrle and therefore briefly sped up the pace of the Nationalist advance.

The Nationalists' victory in the northern war was highly significant. It took out about a quarter of the Republic's armed forces and freed up the Nationalists' navy – quickly redeployed to put pressure on the Republic's eastern shores.

Republican offensives, June to December 1937

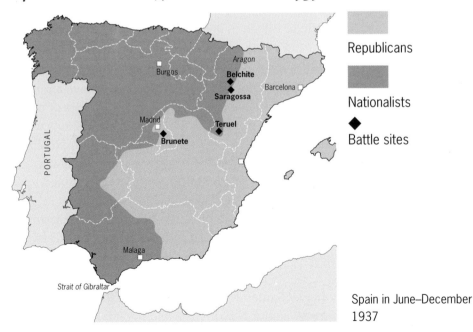

Spain in June–December 1937

During the war in the north, the southern part of the Republic was unable to provide direct help to its northern outpost. Instead, they helped indirectly by launching an offensive of their own in the south. This forced the Nationalists to divide their energies, taking some pressure off the Republic in the north.

On 6 July 1937, 80,000 Republican troops attacked Brunete, the weakest point in the Nationalists' forces encircling Madrid. The offensive was initially highly successful. Franco was unsure how to respond, and took more than a week to plan the counter attack.

Again, Franco decided on a slow and thorough plan which prioritised killing large numbers of Republicans rather than moving swiftly. Once this strategy was implemented the Nationalists halted the Republican advance and, by the end of the offensive, the Republic had lost 25,000 men but had gained only a few miles of territory. This pattern was repeated on the Aragon front in August, where the Republicans recaptured the towns of Belchite and Saragossa in September before being forced back. In December, the **Popular Army** gained Teruel, holding it through the winter only to lose it once again following a Nationalist counter-attack in February.

The failure of the 1937 Republican offensives exposed important weaknesses on the Republican side.

- The Republican militia were better suited to street fighting than **conventional warfare**. Nonetheless, the Republic's strategy was to fight a conventional campaign, inadvertently playing to the strengths of the traditionally trained Nationalists.

- At the same time, whereas the Nationalists had a unified command structure under Franco, the Republicans were weakened by faction fighting. For example, Largo Caballero opposed the Communists' plans for the Brunete offensive. Indeed, he lost his job to **Juan Negrín Lopez** over the question of strategy.

- Franco prolonged the fighting and, in so doing, gave the advantage to his better-trained and more disciplined troops. The Republican forces were not ready for a long war as they did not have the supplies or the training to cope with an extended campaign.

Advance to the Mediterranean, 1938–39

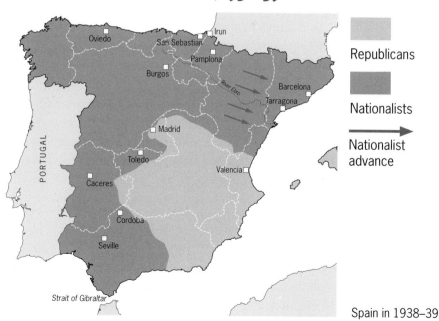

Spain in 1938–39

13-point manifesto

This document set out Negrín's vision for Spain. It proposed a national referendum to allow the Spanish people to decide on their form of government. It also proposed the protection of religious freedom and other civil liberties. Importantly, at the end of the war, Negrín dropped the 13 points and offered to surrender on one condition: that there should be no persecution of Republican supporters under the new regime. Franco, however, rejected even this condition.

Ebro offensive

The Ebro offensive started well. Negrín's generals had organised the campaign, and crossed the River Ebro on pontoons – flat-bottomed boats that can be used as bridges. This tactic caught the Nationalists by surprise and the 80,000 Republican troops made significant gains in the early stages. Franco recognised the seriousness of the attack and ordered a swift counter-attack. For the first time in the war, he personally ordered a new style of tactics, using aircraft to cover advancing infantry and tank divisions. The Republican forces were outnumbered, and running low on equipment, and Franco's new tactics pushed them back.

By the beginning of 1938 it was clear that the Republic could not achieve a military victory. The Nationalists had an army of 600,000, compared to the Republic's 400,000. Additionally, following the war in the north, the Nationalists had far greater resources than the Republicans.

Nonetheless, Negrín refused to surrender. His plan was to keep the war going as long as possible. He hoped that Britain and France would soon declare war on Germany to launch a European war against fascism – including the Nationalist armies of Franco – and in so doing come to the Republic's aid. Negrín had a twofold strategy which he hoped would force Franco to negotiate. First, he published a **13-point manifesto** – a moderate vision for a reunited Spain he hoped Franco would accept. Second, he launched the **Ebro offensive**, which was designed to show that the Republic was still a force to be reckoned with.

Negrín's plan failed.

- Franco refused to negotiate, demanding an unconditional surrender.

- The Ebro offensive, which started well with thousands of Republican troops crossing the River Ebro into Nationalist territory, ended in a Republican retreat. The Republicans did not have the men or resources to maintain their advance.

- News from the rest of Europe was bad: Hitler had invaded Czechoslovakia and yet Britain continued its policy of **appeasement**.

The quickest way for the Nationalists to win the war was to launch yet another attack on Madrid. Franco considered this option, but decided against it as Madrid was still heavily defended. Instead, on 23 December the Nationalists started an assault on Catalonia. The Nationalist campaign was slow. It began with an artillery barrage, and then a steady advance.

The Popular Army, which was smaller, less disciplined and short of supplies after the Ebro offensive, put up little resistance. Franco announced that there would be no forgiveness for former Republicans, and as a result thousands crossed the border into France to escape Nationalist persecution. The Catalonian city of Tarragona fell on 15 January 1939. From this point on, Republican troops could do little to stop the Nationalist advance.

Once Tarragona had fallen, it was clear that the Nationalists would soon conquer Barcelona, the home of Negrín's government. As a result, Negrín and his ministers fled north, to the French border. On 26 January, Barcelona fell to the Nationalists. The fall of Barcelona was highly significant for the Republic. It showed that the Nationalist victory over the whole of Spain was near. As a result, Azaña, who had been President since 1936, resigned and went into exile. On 6 February, what remained of the Cortes met for the last time. Negrín proposed trying to negotiate with Franco; the Cortes agreed. The initiative failed and on 9 February Negrín too fled the country.

The fall of Madrid

Negrín continued to lead the government from exile. He and the Communists were determined to fight on. Senior army leaders, on the other hand, thought that the time had come to negotiate. On 6 March, General Segismundo Casado, the leader of the Republican army, launched a coup against Negrín in Madrid.

Casado's strategy was to break the alliance between the Republic and the PCE, assuming that Franco would negotiate once the Communists had been expelled from government. On hearing of the coup, Negrín phoned General Casado and officially sacked him. However, Negrín was powerless to stop Casado's strategy. As soon as the coup was launched, Casado began arresting Communists. Most of the leaders of the PCE had gone into exile following the fall of Barcelona, and the few who remained were either arrested or imprisoned. This new policy started a new civil war between the part of the army that was loyal to Casado and those who sided with the Communists. Fighting broke out between these different factions and carried on until a ceasefire was agreed on 10 March. The fighting weakened the Republican defence of Madrid. Moreover, General Casado's negotiations with Franco failed. Casado fled, leaving Madrid undefended.

By this time, the Republican army had disintegrated: large sections had surrendered after the fighting between Casado's forces and the Communists had ended. Finally, on 26 March the Nationalist army began a campaign to capture Madrid. A day later, Franco's forces entered the capital. The streets were empty, and the Nationalists faced no opposition. After nearly three years of war, the people of Madrid were in no condition to continue fighting. They simply wanted an end to the war. On 1 April, having conquered Madrid, Franco declared that the war was over.

Conclusion: How did Franco's leadership help the Nationalists to win the civil war?

The Nationalists had considerable advantages over their opponents. First, Franco was able to resolve the tensions among the factions on the Nationalist side. Republican leaders, such as Largo Caballero and Negrín, were never able to unify the communists, liberals and anarchists in the way that Franco unified the Falange, Carlists and monarchists. Second, Franco's army had a disciplined command structure. Indeed, when General Mola disagreed with Sperrle, Franco intervened and settled the matter. Neither Largo Caballero nor Negrín had such authority. Largo Caballero was never able to impose control on Catalonia, and Negrín was betrayed by Casado in the final phases of the war. Third, the Nationalist army was more disciplined and better trained than the hastily thrown-together Popular Army. The militias were excellent street-fighters and therefore resisted the Nationalists in the early days of the war. Nonetheless, Franco's old fashioned tactics prolonged the war, which gave the advantage to the better-trained and organised Nationalist forces. Finally, Franco, commander of the elite Army of Africa, was able to win a string of early successes, which boosted the morale of the Nationalist side. Further successes came during the war in the north and in the final phase of the war, with the victory in Catalonia. In contrast, the Republicans were fighting a defensive war. They rarely had decisive victories and therefore morale on the Republican side dwindled. In sum, Franco's leadership ensured Nationalist unity, military discipline, successes in battle, sustained morale and, finally, victory.

Glossary

Appeasement

A policy of the British government in the 1930s, which sought to avoid war with Hitler by allowing Germany to rearm and expand its territory in Eastern Europe.

Take note

Now that you have read about the whole course of the Spanish Civil War, make three lists:
- Reasons why the Nationalists won.
- Reasons why the Republicans lost.
- The role of Franco. For each list, make a judgment about which reason is most important. Write a paragraph explaining your choice.

Taking it further

Consider the following question: 'Did the Republicans lose, or the Nationalists win, the Spanish Civil War?'
On the surface, this question could seem confusing – the two scenarios are not mutually exclusive. However, considered more carefully, this question is more complex. It is asking whether the outcome of the Spanish Civil War was more a result of Republican errors or Nationalist strengths. For example, were there points at which the Republicans failed to take action which could have swayed the war in their favour? Or were the Nationalists so strong that Republican defeat was assured?
Look back at your notes from this chapter, and the graph you drew as part of the activity. Write a paragraph in answer to this question.

Activity: Turning points

Copy the following axes onto a large sheet of paper:

Nationalist success	
	1936———1937———1938———1939———
Repubican success	

Write each of the events from the timeline at the beginning of this chapter onto a small card. Place these in the relevant place along the *x*-axis.

- Now decide a) whether each event represented a success for the Nationalists or the Republicans, and b) how far it represented a success for the relevant side. Move each small card up or down the *y*-axis accordingly.

- Once you have placed each small card, stick them in place and draw a line connecting the cards. This line represents the course of the Spanish Civil War.

- Finally, choose three events on the graph that you feel represent key turning points in the war. Next to each point, write three sentences explaining your choice.

Activity: Podcasting

Divide into four groups. Using sound recording software, each group should make a two-minute podcast describing one stage of the civil war. Each group should do a different stage. Each podcast should contain a description of the event of the relevant stage and an analysis of how the events affected the outcome of the civil war. Your podcast could be made more interesting in the following ways:

- You could incorporate excerpts from sources read in different voices.

- You could mix in sound effects to illustrate the events that you are describing – there are free online sound effect archives that you could browse.

- You could stage a question-and-answer style interview to facilitate the analysis.

Chapter 7: **Foreign intervention**

Key questions

- What was the impact of the Non-Intervention Pact on the Spanish Civil War?
- In what ways did foreign countries provide aid to the Nationalists and the Republicans during the Spanish Civil War?
- How far did foreign intervention play a decisive role in the outcome of the Spanish Civil War?

From the very start, foreign powers played a significant role in the Spanish Civil War. The Nationalists were aided by the German Nazis and the Italian Fascists, while the democratic Republic was supported by the Russian communists. This fight between democracy and communism on the one side, and fascism on the other, prefigured the battle lines of the Second World War, leading some historians to comment that the Spanish Civil War was 'the world war in miniature'.

Timeline

1936	August	Non-intervention Pact signed by France, Britain and others
	September	Lieutenant Colonel Warlimont arrived as the German commander and military adviser to General Franco
	October	Russian tanks and aircraft arrived to support the Republic
	November	International Brigades arrived to reinforce the Republican Army; Hitler approved formation of the Condor Legion
	December	Mussolini's Italy started supplying the Nationalists with equipment
1937	March	Formation of the Italian Corps; Battle of Guadalajara

Take note

As you read through this chapter, complete the 'International support' sections of your 'Who supported who in the Spanish Civil War?' table.

Intervention and non-intervention

At the beginning of the war, neither side was equipped for a long conflict. As a result, the Republicans and the Nationalists sought foreign aid. Officially, no major power sent military assistance. But, unofficially, arms from Germany, Italy and Russia flooded into Spain. These had a crucial impact on the outcome of the war.

As soon as the war broke out, Republican leaders contacted the French government asking for aid. **Léon Blum** immediately agreed to send aircraft and artillery to help the Republic. Franco's call for aid was also successful, and Germany hastily dispatched military equipment to help the Nationalists. Italy also agreed to supply Franco with aid. Both Germany and Italy were planning to go to war in Europe some time in the next decade, and therefore they were keen to establish Spain as an ally.

But Britain was worried. The British government feared that international involvement in Spain might lead to a war in Europe – a second world war – which Britain was in no position to win. Therefore, the British refused to get involved themselves and advised France to pull out. Britain's decision forced France to rethink.

Biography

Léon Blum

1872–1950

A French politician who served as Prime Minister of France on three occasions, Blum was associated with the Popular Front, a French movement uniting socialists and communists against the threat of a Nazi uprising in France. As head of a Popular Front government himself, Blum was understandably sympathetic to the Spanish Popular Front government.

France also feared a war in Europe, and the French government knew that it could not win a war against Germany and Italy without Britain's help. Consequently, Blum proposed a new idea: a non-intervention pact. 27 countries, including Britain, Germany, the USA, Italy and Russia, agreed to the French plan and publicly committed themselves to send no aid to either side. Privately, Blum acknowledged that non-intervention was not a heroic plan, but it would stop German and Italian aid to the Nationalists and therefore give the Republic a fighting chance.

German and Italian intervention

> **Take note**
>
> Copy the following table:
>
> | | Where did the aid come from? | Details of this aid | Strengths of this aid | Limitations of this aid |
> |---|---|---|---|---|
> | **Republicans** | Aid from Russia | | | |
> | | International Brigades | | | |
> | **Nationalists** | Aid from Germany | | | |
> | | Aid from Italy | | | |
>
> As you read through this and the next two sections, complete the column entitled 'Details of this aid'. Remember to include statistics where possible – examiners love statistics!

Bomber of the German Condor Legion, 1939

Hitler saw the Non-Intervention Pact as a sign of British and French weakness. So, after signing the agreement, he increased the amount of equipment that he sent to Franco. Mussolini did the same. This was a clear breach of the Non-Intervention Pact, but Britain chose to ignore it. As a result, Hitler and Mussolini became even bolder. In both countries the press publicised their aid to Franco.

Overall, aid to the Nationalists was substantial. By July 1936, Franco had bought 6000 rifles, 450 machine guns, 5 million bullets and 10,000 grenades from Germany. In addition, over the course of the war, Germany and Italy supplied Franco with 1300 aeroplanes – including the Condor Legion – a force almost as big as the entire RAF. In December, naval aid was also agreed. German ships would join Nationalist ones in the Atlantic, whilst Italian ships would serve the Nationalists in the Mediterranean. In the first three months of the war, Italy provided Franco with 130 aircraft, 2500 tonnes of bombs, 500 artillery pieces, 700 mortars, 12,000 machine-guns and almost 4000 vehicles. Germany was reluctant to send ground troops, but Italy was more willing. From March 1937, Italy sent 75,000 volunteers – the *Corpo Truppe Volontarie* – to fight alongside the Nationalists.

Russian aid

In response to the actions of Germany and Italy, Russia too broke the terms of the Non-Intervention Pact. Indeed, **Stalin** found two methods of supporting the Republicans. First, he sent **humanitarian aid**.

Biography

Josef Stalin
1878–1953

A Russian communist and leader of the USSR from the late 1920s to 1953. He rose to power after beating his rival, Leon Trotsky, and subsequently persecuted communists who had previously followed Trotsky. He was responsible for the deaths of millions of people during the Great Terror (1936–38).

Glossary

Humanitarian aid
Aid to help civilians who are suffering due to major emergencies such as war.

Stalin claimed that this aid came from the 12,145,000 roubles (the equivalent of half a million pounds at the time) given 'voluntarily' by the Russian people. As the aid came from the people, and as it was not military aid, it did not breach the Non-Intervention Pact.

Secondly, the Russian government sent military assistance, but this was done in secret. The first consignment – consisting of 500 tonnes of military hardware and 1000 tonnes of ammunition accompanied by 500 engineers – arrived in October 1936, just in time to save Madrid from the Nationalists. The Russians continued to supply the Republicans with military equipment until 1939, sending a total of 1500 aeroplanes and about 850 people during the course of the war.

The International Brigades

Foreign assistance also reached the Republic in the form of the International Brigades: men and women from across the globe who were prepared to fight to defend the Republic. These volunteers were organised by **Comintern**, which had branches all over the world. In total, around 35,000 peopled joined the International Brigades. Of these, about 9000 came from France, 2800 from the USA, and 2000 from Britain. Other countries sending volunteers included Finland, Canada, Ireland and Mexico.

Members of the International Brigades fought for political reasons. They tended to view Franco as a **fascist**, and joined the brigades in an attempt to stop the spread of fascism. Some volunteers, such as the 3350 from Italy and the 3000 from Germany, had lost the fight against fascism at home but wanted to stop its rise in Spain. Others wanted to stop fascism because of its link to racism and **imperialism**. For example, about a quarter of the soldiers were Jews who fought to stop the spread of Nazi style anti-Semitism. Similarly, 90 of the American soldiers were black. Black Americans were engaged in their own struggle against racism in the United States. Also, following the Italian invasion of Abyssinia (now Ethiopia), black radicals started to associate fascism with the oppression of black people in Africa. **Oliver Law** is perhaps the best known black American soldier in the International Brigades. He was a communist who had led demonstrations against Italy's invasion of Abyssinia. For Law, the fight against fascism in southern Europe was part of a broader fight against fascism and against the European domination of Africa.

Glossary

Comintern

The Communist International, an organisation established in Russia in 1919 to help bring about communist revolutions in the rest of the world.

Fascism

A radical right-wing ideology, political movement and form of government. Fascists reject the communist belief that human beings should be equal and the liberal belief that human beings should be free. Fascists want to create a social revolution, ending class struggle and reshaping society along military lines. The fascist vision for society includes strict discipline and a common desire to serve the nation rather than individual wants.

Imperialism

The belief that 'civilised' nations should conquer and govern 'less civilised' nations. Imperialism can also refer to the institutions by which one country governs another.

Biography

Oliver Law

1899–1937

A black American political radical and soldier. Law joined the US army in his teens and joined the Communist Party during the Great Depression. He joined one of the International Brigades at the beginning of the Spanish Civil War. It was the first military unit in American history where black and white soldiers fought side by side. He was killed during the battle of Brunete in July 1937.

Oliver Law in 1937

Take note

As you read through the sections on the impact of foreign intervention, complete the final two columns of your table.

The impact of foreign intervention on the Nationalists

Foreign reaction to the civil war benefited the Nationalists much more than it did the Republicans. Primarily, this was because the Nationalists gained from the Non-Intervention Pact. On the one hand, Britain and France refused to aid the Republicans and, on the other hand, they failed to stop German and Italian aid reaching the Nationalists.

Italian and German assistance was crucial in the early part of the war. Their aircraft saved the Nationalists from a possible early defeat by airlifting the Army of Africa to the mainland to reinforce Mola's rebellion.

The Condor Legion – volunteers from the German Air Force – also gave Franco control of the air during the battle in the north in 1937. Furthermore, the arrival of the new German *Messerschmitt* 109 fighters in late 1937 allowed the Nationalists to dominate the skies for the remainder of the war.

Foreign assistance also changed the nature of the war. Prior to the airlift, the conflict was largely restricted to street fighting, with both sides having to improvise and use any weapons they could lay their hands on. However, when the well-trained and disciplined Army of Africa arrived on the mainland equipped with German and Italian weaponry, the Republic had to respond with a similarly well-organised and equipped force. In this way, German and Italian intervention transformed the civil war from disorganised street fighting into a full-scale conflict between rival armies.

In addition to this, foreign aid helped Franco to gain and consolidate his position as Nationalist leader. Unlike Mola, who had initiated the rebellion, Franco was able to obtain aid from Italy and Germany. Furthermore, thanks to the airlift and the equipment provided from overseas, Franco was able to win a string of early victories. While Mola was making slow progress in the north, Franco's Army of Africa advanced more than 500 km in the first four weeks after landing. This gave Franco enormous respect and authority within the Nationalist movement, enabling him to emerge as the undisputed leader.

Finally, German and Italian assistance cost the Nationalists very little. Franco paid for it with long-term loans, making only small repayments during the war itself. Moreover, the Germans interfered very little in Franco's military strategy. The Italians initially demanded a leading role in the Nationalist's battle plans. However, after the dreadful Italian defeat in March 1937 at the **Battle of Guadalajara**, Mussolini placed Italian troops at Franco's command.

The Battle of Guadalajara

Italian commanders tried to show their military superiority by acting independently of the Nationalist army during the Battle of Guadalajara. However, supply problems meant that their tanks were left stranded with no air cover, and those tanks that could move were outclassed by superior Russian tanks. The Italian commanders had no maps and the Italian soldiers were dressed for tropical weather during a harsh Spanish winter. The Italians were trounced, and Mussolini proclaimed that no Italian solider would be allowed back home until the war was won.

The impact of foreign intervention on the Republicans

Russian aid was a mixed blessing to the Republicans. The arrival of Russian aid in October 1936 was highly significant as it ensured that the Republicans could defend Madrid against Nationalist attacks. In the early part of the war, until the arrival of the German *Messerschmitt* 109 fighters in 1937, Russian planes out-performed German and Italian fighters, while Russian tanks – weighing in at 20 tonnes each – were sturdier than the Italian models, which weighed a mere three tonnes. The people of Madrid certainly saw Russia as their saviour and, during the winter of 1936–37, Russian hats, hairstyles and fashion were in vogue in the Spanish capital.

However, Russian aid came at a considerable cost. The Russian government demanded immediate payment in gold for their equipment. In fact, two thirds of Spain's gold, worth $500 million, was shipped to Russia during the war. Additionally, the quality of the materials supplied was often poor, and rarely as good as the German and Italian equipment. Much of the material provided by Russia came from Poland, and the Polish government used the opportunity to sell off its outdated military hardware at extremely high prices.

What is more, the provision of aid allowed Russia considerable influence over the Republican government. Communists were promoted to senior positions, where they used their power to undermine Largo Caballero's military strategy and attack Trotskyites and anarchists. Later, Negrín's government, which depended heavily on Communist support, banned POUM and established a political police force – SIM (*Servicio de Investgación Militar*) – with the aim of removing rivals to the Communists within the Republican zone. In so doing, Negrín and the Communists threatened the unity and effectiveness of the anti-Nationalist forces.

The International Brigades were a huge boost to morale in the Republican territory. However, there were never more than 16,000 International Brigade soldiers in Spain at any one time and therefore they were not a significant factor in the outcome of the war. They were often poorly equipped and poorly trained. **George Orwell**, perhaps the most famous British citizen to fight with the International Brigades, recalled that his rifle 'was a German Mauser dated 1896... It was rusty, the bolt was stiff, the wooden barrel-guard was split; one glance down the muzzle showed that it was corroded and past praying for.'

There were tensions within the International Brigades, as soldiers brought their prejudices with them. British and Irish Brigades, for example, did not work well together due to the historic tensions between the two nations. Co-operation was also hindered by linguistic and cultural differences. In addition, there was political infighting, and the brigades were sometimes caught up in Communist attempts to persecute CNT and POUM supporters. Finally, many in the International Brigades had signed up to take part in a revolutionary war. However, the Communists ran their brigades with traditional military discipline. The infighting and subjection to Communist discipline sapped the International Brigades' effectiveness and will to fight.

Conclusion: What impact did foreign intervention have?

Foreign intervention was crucial to the outcome of the Spanish Civil War. The Non-Intervention Pact failed to stop foreign aid reaching Spain. However, it was significant because it signalled Britain's unwillingness to be involved, and therefore encouraged German and Italian intervention on the Nationalist side. This intervention was highly important in military, political and economic terms. Militarily, the Germans and Italians provided the Nationalists with a large amount of state-of-the-art military hardware. Politically, Franco's ability to obtain a large amount of aid on very good terms enabled him to consolidate his position as leader of the Nationalists.

Biography

George Orwell
1903–1950

A British journalist, novelist and political radical. Born to relatively wealthy parents, Orwell attended Eton, but decided not to go to university. Rather, he pursued a career as a political writer and toured Europe in order to expose the mistreatment of the working class. He went to Spain to fight fascism, where he joined the POUM. He commented 'there aren't so many fascists in the world, so if we all shoot one...' Orwell was seriously wounded at Huesca, and was forced to flee Spain in June 1937 after fighting communist suppression in Barcelona. In 1938, he published a book about his experiences in the Spanish Civil War called *Homage to Catalonia*. His most famous novels are *Nineteen Eighty-four* (1949) and *Animal Farm* (1945).

Take note

Use your graph and annotations from the previous chapter's activity, and your notes on this chapter, to plan an answer to the following question: How far do you agree that, by the end of 1936, Nationalist victory in the Spanish Civil War was assured?

Taking it further

George Orwell is one of the best-known members of the International Brigades. He published his account of his time in Spain in the book *Homage to Catalonia* (1938). Read Chapters 2–7 of his book. These chapters describe his experience of trench warfare in north-east Spain. How far does his account suggest that the brigades played an important role in deciding the outcome of the war? How useful is his account to a historian studying the impact of the International Brigades on the Spanish Civil War?

Activity: Asking for aid

Imagine you are a member of the Republican government in 1938. Write a letter to the British government pleading for aid in your fight against the Nationalists. You should justify your request. You could explain that the Non-Intervention Pact has failed and that German and Italian aid has been extremely helpful to the Nationalists, making a significant impact on the Nationalist war effort. Your letter will be more persuasive if it is clearly structured and contains detailed examples to support your points. Remember to explain your points once you have made them.

Economically, Franco was able to obtain German and Italian aid on credit and therefore there was no risk of the Nationalists going bankrupt. In contrast, Russian aid to the Republicans was much less helpful. The quality of much of the equipment was poor, it was expensive, and it gave the Communists substantial influence within the Republic. In addition, the International Brigades were often ill-equipped and difficult to manage.

At the beginning of the war, both sides looked equally matched. However, the unequal nature of foreign intervention gave the Nationalists the advantage. This indicates that intervention played a decisive role in the outcome of the Spanish Civil War.

Activity: One big essay

Divide into four groups, with each group being allocated one of the following factors that led to Nationalist victory in the Spanish Civil War:

- the strength of international aid to the Nationalists
- the weakness of international aid to the Republicans
- Franco's leadership of the Nationalists
- divisions amongst the Republicans.

Each group should write a paragraph that explains how this factor led to Nationalist victory. They should address the question: 'Why did the Nationalists win the Spanish Civil War?' Each paragraph should:

- begin with a direct answer to the question
- contain at least three specific examples that support the point being made
- and conclude with a sentence that explains why the factor led to Nationalist victory.

Once each group has written their paragraph, the paragraphs should be read aloud so that they form one big essay. As each paragraph is read aloud, the other three groups should assess it using the following criteria:

How clear was the opening paragraph? How detailed and how relevant were the examples? How well did the last sentence explain the importance of their factor?

Activity: Drawing conclusions

When you write essays, it is important that you include specific examples to support the point you are making. It is also important that your conclusion is in line with the argument of your essay.

Copy the conclusion from this chapter onto the middle of a large sheet of paper. Highlight the part that lists the military, political and economic impact of international aid on each side in the war. Use your table from the previous 'Take note' activities to choose a piece of information to support each point made. Write these examples around the edge of the piece of paper, drawing lines to link them to the relevant part of the conclusion.

Chapter 8: **Civilians at war**

Key questions

- What were the key features of life in the Republican and the Nationalist zones?
- How did the civil war impact upon the lives of women?
- What was the impact of political terror on the Spanish population during the civil war?
- How did the experience of civilians shape the outcome of the Spanish Civil War?

Mika Etchebehere was a symbol of revolutionary womanhood during the Spanish Civil war. Following the coup, she took up arms, joining the POUM militia and fighting alongside her husband, Hippolyte. On his death, the men in her squadron turned to her for direction. They elected her leader and followed her into battle against the Nationalists. She fought heroically, frequently encountering danger. On one occasion, she was buried alive under a collapsed building, surviving only because her men dug her out. While she was a hero to the Republic, the Nationalists viewed her as a godless traitor, who had betrayed her country and her sex. However, Etchebehere had the final word. She outlived Franco and, in the year of her death, she published her autobiography *Mi Guerra de Espana – My Spanish War –* which told of her heroic exploits defending socialism during the civil war.

Republicans

Nationalists

Nationalist and Republican
Spain, July 1936

Life in the Republican zone

Republican Spain was split between those who wanted the restoration of the Republican government – including liberals, socialists and communists – and those such as the CNT and POUM who wanted an immediate revolution. This division was evident in the different experiences of civilians in anarchist Catalonia and Republican Madrid (see page 9 on anarchism).

Take note

As you read through the next few sections of this chapter, create a table listing the political, economic and social features of both the Republican and Nationalist zones.

You do not need to include all of the information in these sections. Instead, try the following method of selecting information:

- Read through each section, recording the general points made. General points are the main points made as opposed to the specific information (detailed facts and figures) provided to support those points.
- Consider the general points you have recorded – are any of them similar? Can they be combined to reduce their number? Can you summarise them? Try to ensure that you have no more than three general points per section.
- Note down these general points and then select one specific example to support each one.

Glossary

Collectivised

In the context of the Spanish Civil War, anarchists used this word to describe businesses which had been taken under workers' control. Typically, the workers elected a committee from amongst themselves to run the business on their behalf.

Revolutionary Spain, 1936

Militia member poses in Barcelona, July 1936

Catalonia

The Spanish revolution was at its most radical in Catalonia in the early part of the war. In Barcelona, Catalonia's principle city, working people – many of whom were members of the anarchist CNT – had risen up spontaneously against the government. In its place they created a political, economic and social revolution.

Politics in Barcelona

Politically, the revolution stripped Barcelona's official government of its power. The Catalan government offered to pass control of the region to the CNT (see page 9). However, the CNT remained true to its anarchist principles and refused to form a government. The CNT stated that the people themselves would take control and create a new society, free from the government, from big business and from the Church. To this end, the CNT trade unions took over the running of the city.

The economy in Barcelona

The new politics created an economic revolution. Around 70% of Barcelona's industry – around 2000 businesses – was **collectivised**. In each business, the workers set up democratically elected management committees. The committees organised the factory, setting wage rates and improving working conditions. The former owners were either executed or allowed to stay on under the direction of the workers.

Workers' committees were successful at transforming what they did in order to meet the needs of the war economy. For example, a factory that had produced lipstick was reorganised by a workers' committee in order to produce bullets.

In addition to factories, public services and industrial production were collectivised. Transport, which had ground to a halt while the workers defeated the coup, was also collectivised. Indeed, CNT unions quickly restarted Barcelona's transport infrastructure, getting buses and trams moving and turning private cars into community taxis.

The CNT organised food distribution. CNT lorries travelled to Aragon and bartered manufactured goods for meat and vegetables. Workers in Barcelona could then buy this food using the **vouchers** they had earned working. Indeed, the CNT collectivised the Ritz and workers and soldiers ate there in the finest restaurant in the region.

Society in Catalonia

Catalonia was also swept by a social revolution. Symbols of the old way of life were attacked. Churches were burnt or turned into hospitals, statues of Jesus were pulled down and prisons were opened, releasing their inmates. In the early days, the revolution even affected the smallest details of people's lives. Suits and ties, which were associated with the old rulers, disappeared and people dressed in blue overalls, the clothes of factory workers. People no longer used words such as 'señor' ('sir'), which implied that one person was more important than another. Rather they called each other 'comrade'.

> ### George Orwell describes revolutionary Barcelona in December 1936
>
> "It was the first time that I had ever been in a town where the working class was in the saddle. Practically every building of any size had been seized by the workers and was draped with red flags* or with the red and black flag of the anarchists; every wall was scrawled with the hammer and sickle and with the initials of the revolutionary parties; almost every church had been gutted and its images burnt. Churches here and there were being systematically demolished by gangs of workmen. Every shop and cafe had an inscription saying that it had been collectivised; even the bootblacks [shoe-polishers] had been collectivised and their boxes painted red and black. Waiters and shop-walkers looked you in the face and treated you as an equal. In outward appearance it was a town in which the wealthy classes had practically ceased to exist. Except for a small number of women and foreigners there were no 'well-dressed' people at all. Practically everyone wore rough working-class clothes, or blue overalls, or some variant of the militia uniform."
>
> * POUM fought under the Russian communist flag – a red flag with a hammer and sickle.

Aragon

In Aragon, an agricultural province just west of Catalonia, peasants did the same as their Catalan cousins. They rose up and seized the land that they worked. Here, too, central government was abolished. In its place the peasants set up the council of Aragon to organise a defence against the Nationalists. The council was highly democratic. It was made up of peasants representing the various farms and workshops across Aragon, and the representatives enjoyed no special privileges.

Local committees organised food rationing. Each person received a free, equal share – 100 g of sugar, meat and rice per day – whilst coffee and cigarettes were given away for free. Eventually cigarettes had to be rationed due to the high demand.

The impact of the revolution in Catalonia and Aragon on the war effort

The political and economic revolution had a significant impact on the war effort. Following the Nationalist coup, the Republican government had lost control of Catalonia and Aragon. The anarchists quickly restored order, restarted production, and transformed their industries to meet the needs of the war.

Glossary

Vouchers

Across Barcelona and Aragon, money was abolished and replaced with vouchers. Workers earned one voucher for every hour of work that they did. This created a more equal society as people received the same payment regardless of the job they did.

Orwell's brigade in 1937

What is more, collectivisation gave the workers an incentive to continue production and therefore aided the swift recovery of the economy after the coup. The social revolution also aided the war effort because working people felt committed to the new, more equal society, and were therefore prepared to fight to defend it. However, in the long-run, the political and economic revolution was to cause conflict between Catalonia and Madrid.

Republican Madrid

The revolution was far less radical in Madrid. In the capital, the central government had a much greater degree of control. Similarly, the economy was run along more traditional lines. Only 30% of Madrid's industries were collectivised and money remained part of everyday life.

For most of the war, Madrid was under siege from the Nationalists and daily life was dominated by Nationalist attacks. Initially, the capital's citizens dug trenches and set up barricades in order to resist the attack. As the war went on, Nationalist bombing raids caused extreme disruption to day-to-day life. The first bombing raid, which took place on 28 August 1936, led to the formation of residents committees which organised blackouts and air raid shelters. Additionally, food shortages and long queues became a fact of life during the war. In spite of these difficulties, the people of Madrid were determined to fight on. This spirit was captured in the slogan '¡No pasarán!', meaning 'They shall not pass!'

The mood of Madrid's citizens changed as the war progressed. Largo Caballero responded to the Nationalist threat by relocating the Republican government to Valencia in November 1936. As a result, many believed that Madrid would soon be lost to the Nationalists, and morale fell.

The fall of the Spanish revolution

During 1937, the Republican government slowly regained control of Catalonia. As this happened, the revolutionary culture of Catalonia disappeared.

When George Orwell returned to Catalonia in April 1937, he noted that the anarchist militia had been replaced by the government-controlled Popular Army. Unlike the militia, the Popular Army had a traditional hierarchy in which officers enjoyed more pay and privileges than the men they led. Divisions between rich and poor had also re-emerged. Money had been reintroduced and goods were bought and sold in the traditional way, replacing the CNT's food distribution system which had tried to ensure that everyone got what they needed. As a result, the poorest lived in poverty whilst the rich could get whatever they wanted on the **black market**.

Workers' control finally came to an end in Barcelona in May 1937. Government and Communist forces arrived at the Barcelona telephone exchange to take back control from the CNT. Fighting broke out, with the anarchist CNT and the Trotskyite POUM fighting against the Republicans and the Communists. After a couple of days, both sides agreed to withdraw in order to end the violence.

American writer Martha Gellhorn on everyday life in wartime Madrid

"You would be walking down a street, hearing only the city noises of streetcars and automobiles and people calling to one another, and suddenly, crushing it all out, would be the huge deep booming of a falling shell, at the corner. There was no place to run."

Glossary

Black market

The buying and selling of illegal goods, often for inflated prices.

However, the government broke its promise and its troops returned to the city to arrest members of the CNT and POUM. On 16 June, POUM was officially banned and, in late June, much of the POUM leadership were executed by Spanish communists. Anarchy lasted longer in Aragon. However, on 4 August, 11,000 Popular Army troops were sent in to crush the peasants' council. The council was officially dissolved on 11 August 1937.

In *Homage to Catalonia*, Orwell claimed that the repression of the workers' movement sapped Barcelona's will to fight and was responsible for Barcelona's fall to the Nationalists. The workers were willing to fight for the revolution, but were less willing to fight for the Republic.

Women in Republican Spain

Women in the Republican zone enjoyed unprecedented freedoms and played a highly significant role in the Republican war effort. At the top of government, the communist **Dolores Ibárruri**, who was known as *La Pasionaria* (the passion flower), played an important role in boosting morale in war-torn Madrid. Her powerful speeches in the Spanish Parliament and at public meetings, urging the people of Madrid to fight on, were widely reported. Federica Montseny, a well-known anarchist, joined Largo Caballero's government as Minister of Health. In this role she introduced special clinics for women, and was behind the legalisation of abortion in the Republican zone.

In the first weeks of the war, some women joined the communist and anarchist militias and fought on the front lines. Indeed, the POUM militia encouraged women to join, stating that their policy was to share assignments – even those traditionally associated with women, such as washing clothes – equally between both sexes.

Although the total number of women who fought in the militias is thought to be less than 1000, a few, including Mika Etchebehere, played a leading role. Initially, Etchebehere served under her husband Hippolyte in a battalion of the POUM militia, fighting Mola's forces to the north of Madrid. On her husband's death, Etchebehere took over the leadership of the unit.

The anarchists and the communists both set up women's organisations. The anarchist group *Mujeres Libres* (Free Women) had around 20,000 members. The group fought to end prostitution, which they believed was an extreme form of female exploitation. They offered training to women who wanted to stop working as prostitutes and start a new life. They also patrolled red light districts in Catalonia and shot pimps on sight. In Barcelona, the CNT worked to phase out brothels. The expensive brothels were closed immediately, and brothels in working-class areas were collectivised – that is to say, the prostitutes themselves took control.

> ### Excerpt from Mary Low and Juan Brea, *Red Spanish Notebook* (1979)
> "In the end, the prostitutes began to look after their own interests, they realised that they too could be in the revolution. Immediately they occupied their 'working premises'. They proclaimed their equality and formed a trade-union. All profits were equally shared. A framed notice was hung up in every brothel announcing 'You are expected to treat the women as comrades.'"

Biography

Dolores Ibárruri
1895–1989

The best-known female Republican leader during the Spanish Civil War. She grew up in the Basque region and was the daughter of a mine-worker. She became a revolutionary in the 1920s and, in the 1930s, wrote for the newspaper of the Spanish Communist Party. During the civil war she was considered to be the most inspiring speaker on the Republican side. Her slogan, *"No Pasarán"* became the most well-known of the civil war. She was exiled following the Nationalist victory but returned to Spain two years after Franco's death.

Excerpt from *The Times*, 25 July 1936, on women in Republican Valencia

"Corps of militia-women have been organised, and women, armed and aggressive, take their place in the front line with men. All that womanhood traditionally stands for is rapidly disappearing."

The Communists organised the AMA (Women against Fascism). This mobilised women to help the war effort, but tended to emphasise traditional roles. The 50,000 members of the AMA worked as nurses, and organised crèches and orphanages. The crèches were significant as, not only did they employ women, they also played a role in allowing women with children to join the labour force themselves.

Overall, the civil war was a time of liberation for many women in the Republican zone. Nonetheless, there was never complete sexual equality. The Republican government continued to use stereotypical images of women. Some posters emphasised that women were vulnerable and needed the protection of men, and official propaganda about working women focused on images of young, conventionally beautiful women.

Life in the Nationalist zone

There was a big contrast between life in the Republican zone and conditions under the Nationalists. While the military coup had weakened or destroyed central authority in Republican areas, the Nationalist's control of the army gave them unrivalled power in their territory. On 18 July, the Nationalists imposed **martial law**, which gave the army almost total power over everyday life in their zone. Having gained control, the Nationalists introduced a series of measures which rolled back the reforms of the Second Republic and re-established Spanish tradition.

- The Nationalists banned all of the political parties that had opposed the coup. CEDA, which had supported the coup, dissolved itself voluntarily in April 1937. At the same time, Franco set up a new political party, the *Falange Española Tradicionalista y de law – Junta de Ofensiva Nacional Sindicalista* (FET-JONS), which amalgamated the various different Nationalist political groups and placed them under his control. Following the Decree of Unification of 19 April 1937, all other political parties were outlawed and FET-JONS became the only legal political party in the Nationalist zone.

- The Nationalists also banned strikes and abolished independent trade unions. Franco's March 1938 Labour Charter set up a state-run replacement for the trade unions: the Spanish Syndical Organisation (OS). However, unlike the old unions, the OS was responsible to the government rather than its members. These measures effectively made factory owners much more powerful and reduced the rights of working people.

- In rural areas, the land reforms that had happened since 1931 were all abolished. This policy passed power, privilege and wealth back to the traditional landowners at the expense of the peasants.

The role of the Church

The Spanish Church also enjoyed a special position in the Nationalist zone. At the time of the rebellion, the Church backed neither the Nationalists nor the Republicans. But, in September 1936, Cardinal Enrique Pla y Deniel, the Bishop of Salamanca, published a letter entitled *The Two Cities*, backing the Nationalist **crusade** against the 'godless communism' of the Republic.

Glossary

Martial law

A situation in which the normal police force is replaced by the army. Under martial law, the army usually has much greater powers than the normal police force.

Crusade

A holy war.

Franco wanted the Church to play a unifying role in Nationalist Spain. He hoped that the Church's teaching, backed by military power, would create a 'Christian civilisation' based on traditional morality.

The Church was also given a special role in Nationalist education. In Cordoba, the Commission for Purging Public Education sacked teachers who were sympathetic to the Republic. On 1 October 1936, crucifixes were reintroduced into all classrooms in the Nationalist zone as a symbol of the Church's authority. In 1938, **co-education** was abolished, meaning that male and female students were educated separately, with female students taught by female teachers and male students by male teachers.

Society in Nationalist Spain

Nationalist Spain did have its lighter side. Military parades, bands and militia men marching in formation and singing hymns did much to lift the morale of Nationalists during the war. There was also an emphasis on religious and military pageantry, with colourful uniforms and ceremonial robes playing a big part in official festivals.

Additionally, people were generally better off in the Nationalist zone.

- The Nationalists occupied the major farming regions in Spain, including Extremadura, and therefore they could produce enough food for the population.

- Franco bought Italian and German arms on credit, which meant that the Nationalists had money to spend on consumer goods.

- The Nationalists controlled the Canary Islands, which contained Spain's largest tobacco farms. Therefore, cigarettes were cheaper and more plentiful than in the Republican zone. This was significant as smoking was very popular at the time.

Men and women under the Nationalists

The Nationalists quickly reasserted traditional gender roles. Men were expected to be obviously macho, and serve in either the local militia or the Nationalist army. Men who refused, or criticised the emphasis on the military, were publicly ridiculed, imprisoned or executed.

Women were also under intense pressure to conform to their allotted role. The Spanish Catholic Church had traditionally taught that women were intellectually, physically and morally weaker than men. According to the Church, and Franco's government, women were supposed to look after the home for their father or their husband. On a day-to-day basis, women were expected to dress simply: this meant no lipstick or make up, and wearing trousers was forbidden.

Divorce and homosexuality were outlawed, and sex outside marriage was officially condemned. This did not, however, stop what the Church called 'immoral sexual affairs'. Indeed, the conditions created by the civil war lead to a spectacular rise in prostitution. Women whose husbands died in the war sometimes saw no alternative to prostitution to support themselves, while soldiers who were stationed away from their wives and girlfriends often ignored orders to close brothels and instead made use of them.

Glossary

Co-education

The education of boys and girls in the same institution.

March of a Nation

Daily Mail journalist Harold Cardozo recorded his experiences of Nationalist Spain in his book, *March of a Nation* (1937).

"...my favourite parades were the Carlists and the Falangists. The first were so cheerful and dashing with their scarlet berets, their khaki shirts, wide open on the chest, their shining equipment, and their white socks so neatly rolled round the ankle over their cord-soled shoes. The second in their blue uniforms, looked workman-like, and they sang their Falangist hymn so passionately as they marched!"

Nonetheless, the civil war did provide women with opportunities to play a role in public life. Women could join all-female political groups such as the Carlist *Margaritas* or the Falange's *Sección Femenina* (SF). By 1939, the SF had 580,000 members doing a variety of social work. For example, they organised orphanages, and distributed bread and soup to the poor. Often the SF distributed food in areas that had recently been captured by the Nationalists. In this sense, they were part of Franco's propaganda campaign and attempted to persuade people in newly conquered territories that life would be better under the Nationalists. The *Margaritas* also helped the war effort by organising hospitals near the front line to look after wounded Nationalist soldiers.

As the majority of men were serving in the army, women could also contribute to the war effort by making munitions. However, the work that women did was unpaid, and in this sense it did nothing to make them financially independent.

Political terror

The Nationalists and Republicans both used **political terror** against their enemies. The exact numbers killed on both sides may never be known, but it is estimated that the Republican Red Terror killed between 38,000 and 55,000 people and the Nationalist White Terror between 150,000 and 200,000.

The Red Terror was very different from the White Terror. In the Republican zone, the killings of priests, landlords, factory owners, Falangists and members of CEDA happened largely at the beginning of the war when the Republican government had lost control and was powerless to stop the violence. In fact, once order was restored in the Republican zone, the number of killings dropped sharply as the CNT in Catalonia and the government in Madrid worked to stop political violence. However, in the Nationalist zone, the terror was part of official policy. From the start, Franco could have stopped the killings of socialists, anarchists, homosexuals and trade unionists, but instead he encouraged it.

The Red Terror

In the Republican zone, the main victims of the terror were people associated with Spain's traditional rulers. For example, Republican militias killed around 7000 priests during the war. Similarly, in Catalonia, the terror turned against factory owners, and in Aragon landowners were killed in large numbers. In Republican cities, local militias were known for executing people in nightly raids. These raids involved arresting a suspected Nationalist sympathiser and then transporting them out of town, where they would be executed. The victims were often humiliated during their execution. For example, the local priest in Cienpozuelos was thrown into the **bull ring** and, in Ciudad Real, the priest was castrated and his genitals stuffed in his mouth. Buildings associated with the old elites were also destroyed. In Barcelona only one of the city's 58 churches survived the revolution.

But, by the winter of 1936, the Red Terror was essentially over. In Madrid, the Republican government halted the violence by setting up tribunals to ensure that people received a trial. In Catalonia, too, the CNT set up revolutionary courts to curb the violence.

Take note

As you read through this section, complete two spider diagrams – one for the Republican (Red) Terror and one for the Nationalist (White) Terror – use the headings 'atrocities', 'impact' and 'victims'.

Glossary

Political terror

A term used to describe violent acts against the people designed to discourage and eliminate political opposition.

Bull ring

An arena in which bull-fighting takes place.

Although only short-lived, the Red Terror had a significant impact on the course of the war. The attack on the Church helped to persuade senior Church leaders to back the Nationalists. Internationally, the terror persuaded the Vatican and the wider Catholic community to side with the Nationalists and gave the British a pretext for refusing to support the Republicans. Finally, the Nationalists publicised Republican violence and used it in a propaganda campaign against the old government. This was highly effective due to the strongly held religious faith of many in the Nationalist zone.

The White Terror

The White Terror was, in part, an attempt to consolidate Nationalist rule by removing political opponents. It was also a moral crusade against those perceived to be enemies of Catholic Spain. Nationalists used terror throughout the war. After every victory, the Falange, backed by the military, rounded up supporters of the Republic, humiliated them and executed them.

In the first weeks of the war, the terror focused on people in positions of power who had opposed the coup. For example, in Andalusia the Nationalists targeted the anarchists who posed a real threat to their power. In other areas, the terror was part of the implementation of Nationalist policies. In Extremadura, 1800 peasants were killed as land was returned to landowners. The bodies of peasants were left unburied in their fields as an example to the rest of their village. The terror accompanied the advance of the Nationalists. For example, the Nationalists killed 4000 residents of Malaga when they captured the town in February 1937.

The White Terror was also a moral crusade. Senior Nationalists described this terror as a 'clean-up operation', which would cleanse Spanish society of moral 'evils' such as independent women and homosexuals. The execution of the famous poet and playwright **Federico Garcia Lorca**, who was known to be homosexual, sent a powerful message that people who chose to live untraditional lives would not be tolerated by the new regime.

The killings were deliberately linked to Church festivals. For example, in Pamplona, the annual celebration of the Virgin Mary in mid-August was accompanied by mass executions. The executions were described in religious language as a 'blood sacrifice' necessary to win God's favour.

Every area won by the Nationalists was purged in order to ensure the Nationalists were unopposed and to root out the moral corruption that Franco would not tolerate in the new Spain. For example, in 1937, immediately after the victory in the Basque region, Franco ordered the execution of several hundred prominent Basque nationalists. Franco's strategy was devious. He persuaded them to surrender by promising them safe passage to England. The Basque leaders boarded two ships bound for Britain. However, Nationalist ships blockaded the port, forcing the refugees back to shore, where they were imprisoned, tried and sentenced to death.

The Terror was particularly cruel in the province of Teruel, which changed hands three times during the war. In the village of Concud, the Nationalists dug a pit six feet wide and 250 feet deep, a mass grave for the 1005 men, women and children whose 'crimes' included being critical of the

Biography

Federico Garcia Lorca

1898–1936

Spanish poet, playwright and theatre director. During the Second Republic, Garcia Lorca became the director of a university theatre company known as 'The Shack'. He was known for touring Spain with his company, performing plays that he had written himself. Sadly, he left the safety of Madrid three days before the outbreak of the civil war and was in a Nationalist area in the early days of the war.

Death toll

It is impossible to know exactly how many people were killed during the Spanish Civil War in total. Nationalist forces suggested 1,000,000 casualties. More recent estimates suggest about half this number. This does not, however, include those who died from the malnutrition, starvation and disease caused by the conflict.

Nationalists, reading liberal newspapers before the war, owning a radio or being related to a Republican supporter.

The White Terror led to a huge increase in Falange membership. Former Republicans and trade unionists joined the Falange in large numbers to show their loyalty to the new regime and avoid execution. As a result, the blue shirts, part of the Falange uniform, were nicknamed 'life-jackets'.

The White Terror claimed as many as 200,000 lives. But, more than that, the killings created an atmosphere of terror which made people in the Nationalist zone suspicious and afraid to speak out.

Conclusion: How did the experience of civilians shape the outcome of the Spanish Civil War?

In the Nationalist zone, the extensive and continuing use of terror allowed Franco to consolidate his power. Moreover, Franco used the support of the Church and propaganda which focused on the atrocities committed in the Republican zone to strengthen support within the Nationalist zone.

By contrast, popular support for the Republican cause diminished over time. Infighting between socialists and communists on the one hand, and anarchists on the other, sapped the strength of the forces that opposed Franco. Indeed, as the Republican government repressed the social revolution in Catalonia and Aragon, the working class and the peasantry became increasingly disillusioned with the Republicans and less willing to fight on their behalf.

In this way, life in the two zones played an important part in the outcome of the Spanish Civil War.

Taking it further

Search the Internet for Spanish Civil War propaganda (you could try typing 'Spanish Civil War propaganda' into a search engine image search). Choose six contrasting images. Make sure that three were produced by the Nationalists and three by the Republicans. Print out these images or import them into an electronic document. Make notes around them to highlight the key features of the Republican message and the key features of the Nationalist message. Try to remember these images when you are revising for your exam – they could be useful examples for your essays.

Fascist parade commemorates the first anniversary of Franco's victory

Activity: Top Secret!

Imagine you are a secret police officer working for the Nationalists. Your job is to root out opposition and impure elements in Spanish society. The following six files have been passed on to you. You must read them carefully and decide who should stand trial as an enemy of Spain.

Name: Juan Suarez
Age: 61
Occupation: Landowner
Details: A devout member of the Catholic Church. A prominent member of CEDA. Devotes a significant proportion of his income to charitable work through the local nunnery. Has a son who is a member of the Falange.

Name: Emilio Lopez
Age: 48
Occupation: Farmer
Details: Born in Extremadura. Little education. Worked the land from an early age. Not interested in politics, but dislikes the Falange as he believes they are 'ungodly' – he is a committed Catholic. Would like to see Spain ruled by a king.

Name: Maria Angelo
Age: 31
Occupation: Factory worker
Details: Brought up a Catholic, but has not attended church since her youth. Boyfriend in the Falange. Wears make-up and reads American fashion magazines. Participated in a strike against the CEDA government in 1934. Joined the SF following the Nationalist occupation of her home town.

Name: Eva Esteban
Age: 20
Occupation: Prostitute
Details: Lives in Barcelona. Was employed by an expensive brothel in the centre of the city, frequented in the past by wealthy businessmen. Following the closure of the brothel, joined the CNT and helped collectivise other brothels in the city. In a relationship with a member of the Popular Army.

Name: Miguel Ferrer
Age: 28
Occupation: Member of POUM militia
Details: Born into a wealthy family. Joined PSOE in 1934 but following the coup joined the POUM militia to defend Barcelona from the Nationalists. Works in the central Barcelona telephone collective and has been accused of listening in to government communications.

Name: Xavier Fernandez
Age: 54
Occupation: Teacher
Details: Born into a lower-middle-class family. Joined the army at the age of 15. Worked with the army in 1934 suppressing the anarchist revolt in Asturias. Invalided out of the army. Divorced his wife. Became an outspoken critic of the Republican army and joined the Carlist militia.

- Make notes on each file, indicating which elements of their biography are suspicious, and which indicate that they can be trusted. For each case, make a recommendation for further action and write a sentence justifying it. Remember to watch out for people wearing 'life-jackets' (i.e. people involved in Republican activities before the civil war, but now working with the Nationalists) – do you think they can really be trusted?

- Now repeat the activity. This time, examine the files in your role as a member of the CNT militia. Again, make recommendations about who should face a revolutionary tribunal and who is a reliable comrade.

- Finally, repeat the activity as a member of SIM (see page 57). Your priority is to root out enemies of the Republic within the Republican zone.

Skills Builder 3: **Writing introductions and conclusions**

When answering questions in Unit 1, students will be expected to write an essay. In this third Skills Builder, we will be looking at the importance of writing introductory and concluding paragraphs.

When writing under examination conditions, you should spend approximately 40 minutes on the whole of your essay. During this time you must:

- plan what you are going to write
- write a separate paragraph for each major point you wish to make
- check through what you have written.

Therefore, given the time constraints, you should not spend more than five minutes writing your introduction.

What should you put in your introduction?

Your introduction should answer the question directly and set out what you plan to cover and discuss in your essay. Your introduction needs to show that you will answer the question in an analytical way – and that you haven't just started writing without thinking. Therefore, it is good to say, very briefly, what you are going to argue in the essay. You can then refer back to your introduction as you write, to make sure that your argument is on track.

We are going to look at an introduction to an answer to the following question:

> (A) How far do you agree that foreign intervention was the main reason why the Nationalists won the Spanish Civil War, 1936–39?

This question gives one of the commonly stated reasons for Nationalist victory, and it asks you 'how far' you agree that it was the most important reason. This will require you to assess other reasons why the Nationalists won and make judgments about the significance of each reason in bringing it about.

Here is an example of an introduction that you might write:

Foreign intervention was one of the reasons why the Nationalists won the Spanish Civil War, but there were also other factors behind their victory. Franco's leadership, divisions within the Republican side and the attitude of Britain, France and other countries that did not intervene also played an important part in the outcome of the war. Nonetheless, foreign intervention was the most important factor because it gave the Nationalists access to a greater quantity and a better quality of resources than the Republicans, and in this way offset the advantages that the Republicans had at the beginning of the war.

This introduction answers the question directly. It recognises that there were a number of causes behind the Nationalist victory. It states some of these causes, and it briefly explains why foreign intervention was the most important factor.

Activity: **Spot the mistake**

The following introductions have been written in response to Question (A). Each one illustrates a common mistake. Spot them!

Example 1

The Spanish Civil War started in 1936 due to the failure of the Second Republic. The Second Republic was established in 1931 and was a beacon of hope for those people in Spain who hoped that it would bring about much needed reform. However, supporters of the Church, rich land owners and a significant section of the army feared that democracy would lead to communism and by the middle of 1936 it was clear that a civil war was inevitable. This essay will consider why the Nationalists won.

Example 2

Foreign intervention was vital to Nationalist success in the civil war. The Germans and Italians provided men and equipment to the Nationalists that they would not have had. German aircraft, in the form of the Condor Legion, were particularly useful, as they gave the Nationalists control of the air. The Italians also sent tanks and over 80,000 men. What is more, Franco didn't have to pay for this aid during the war due to generous credit agreements. Russian aid to the Republicans was poor by contrast. Often the Russians provided weapons that were out of date and forced the Republicans to pay for this aid in advance in gold. That is why foreign intervention helped the Nationalists to win.

Example 3

The most important factor which explains the victory of the Nationalists was political leadership. The Nationalists were united under Franco from a very early point in the war. The Republicans, on the other hand, were disunited. Anarchists controlled Catalonia, whilst an alliance of socialists, communists and liberals controlled Madrid. These political factors are the reason why Franco won in the end.

Answers

Example 1 – this introduction sets out the background to the civil war rather than answering the question.

Example 2 – this introduction focuses on the stated factor and the nature of the aid, not considering any other factors.

Example 3 – this introduction only considers one possible factor and therefore is highly unbalanced. Moreover, it ignores the stated factor.

It is important to link each of your paragraphs to the introduction. So, for Question (A), you could provide evidence in paragraph 2 that explains the importance of Franco's leadership. Then, in paragraph 3, you could show how far Republican divisions hampered their war effort. In paragraph 4, you could focus on the significance of British and French inaction.

It is important that your essay does not contradict your introduction. If you state in your introduction that foreign intervention was the most important factor, then you must maintain this argument throughout your essay.

Why are conclusions important?

When you are asked a question in an examination, you are expected to answer it! The concluding paragraph is very important in this process. It should contain the summary of the argument you have made, with your verdict on the question.

Like an introduction, the conclusion should not be more than three or four sentences in length, and under examination conditions it should take no more than five minutes to write. Here is an example of a conclusion for Question (A):

Foreign intervention was the most important factor in deciding the outcome of the Spanish Civil War as supplies of equipment, troops, specialists and credit clearly gave the Nationalists an advantage over their opponents. Additionally, foreign intervention increased the political difficulties of the Republic because aid from communist Russia led to increased communist influence in the Republican government and therefore to purges of anarchists and Trotskyites which weakened Republican fighting strength. Foreign aid also strengthened Franco's position as leader of the Nationalists because he alone had been able to secure the aid, on excellent terms. British and French non-intervention was important, but mainly because it allowed Germany and Italy the freedom to support Franco as they chose.

Write a conclusion of not more than four sentences to the following question:

> (B) How far do you agree that the Nationalist victory in the Spanish Civil War was inevitable from the start?

Try to write it in no more than five minutes.

Chapter 9: **Spain under Franco, 1939–56**

Key questions

- How did Franco consolidate his power in the period 1939–45?
- What were the key features of Franco's foreign policy in the period 1939–56?
- What were the key features of Franco's social and economic policies in the period 1939–56?

Even Franco's closest associates thought he was mysterious. He came from the Spanish region of Galicia and, according to folklore, the people of that region were so mysterious that if you met them on the stairs it was impossible to tell if they were going up or down. Following the civil war, Franco's plans for Spain were also mysterious. How would he deal with former Republicans? Would he create a fascist state? Would he give up power and restore the monarchy? What role would Spain play in the Second World War? Franco was in no hurry to answer these questions. In fact, his willingness to keep people guessing was one of the secrets of his power.

Francisco Franco in 1944

Timeline

March–April 1938	Clerical Laws; Press Law; Reintroduction of 1889 Civil Code
February 1939	Law of Political Responsibilities
October 1940	Franco and Hitler met to discuss Spain's entry into the Second World War
June 1945	Spain excluded from membership of the United Nations
June 1947	Law of Leadership Succession
April 1948	US President Truman authorised the Marshall Plan. Spain excluded
February 1949	America begins a series of loans to Spain
August 1953	Spanish concordat with the Vatican
September 1953	Treaty of Madrid
July 1954	Vagrancy Act
December 1955	Spain joined the United Nations

Take note

Broadly, Franco used four methods to strengthen his hold over Spain: conciliation, repression, propaganda and political manipulation.

Fold a piece of A4 paper into quarters. Open the paper out again and label the four quarters:

- conciliation
- repression
- propaganda
- political manipulation.

As you read through this section, list his actions under these four headings. Once you have completed this task, you could use your notes to plan an answer to the question: 'How far did Franco use repression to consolidate his power in the period 1939–45?'

The Nationalists had won the civil war but the new government was forced to deal with the legacy of the war. For Franco, this meant continued terror to stamp his authority on every area of Spanish life, and economic reconstruction to rebuild the country. In addition, Spanish foreign policy was shaped by the legacy of German and Italian aid which had been instrumental in Nationalist victory in the civil war.

The consolidation of power, 1939–45

Franco's regime – the New State – was born during the civil war and it maintained a warlike character for some time afterwards. The war's legacy was evident in Franco's two main domestic aims: to establish control and to root out opposition through terror.

Establishing control

During the war, the Nationalist coalition of traditional monarchists, Falangists and Carlists had worked together to ensure victory. Following Franco's victory, there were immediate tensions within the coalition concerning the future of the regime. Franco, however, had his own agenda and was unwilling to give power away to any of the Nationalist factions.

The monarchists were perhaps the biggest threat to Franco. There was genuine popular support for the restoration of a monarch as a way of reuniting Spain after the war. Franco's strategy for dealing with the monarchists was to agree that the monarchy would be restored, but at the same time to emphasise that this would happen 'at the right time'. Indeed, he contacted **Don Juan**, the Spanish king in exile, to promise that, in due course, he would be King of Spain. However, Franco argued that the problems created by the civil war and the outbreak of the Second World War in 1939 meant that Spain was vulnerable to attack and, therefore, for the time being, it was important to have an experienced military commander in power. In 1947 he passed the Law of Leadership Succession which formally declared that Spain was a monarchy. However, the law did not state who the king would be, and left the decision and the timing of that decision to Franco.

Although they had no desire for a monarchy, the Falange lent their support to Franco. They hoped that he would bring about the fascist state they desired. Franco capitalised on their support, giving them important positions in the economy and management of the media. This strengthened Franco's power in two ways: not only did it ensure the loyalty of the Falange, it also denied the monarchists access to methods of creating and distributing propaganda.

The Carlists were of little threat to Franco's power. During the civil war, Franco had merged the Carlist militia with the Falange. Consequently, many Carlists were won over to fascism. They had worked with equipment and soldiers from Germany or Italy and now felt that fascism was a powerful force which could lead to the rebirth of Spain. This left the Carlist leaders with very little popular support.

Glossary

Messiah

The literal meaning is 'God's chosen one'. Christians associate the term with Jesus. Franco used the word to imply that he was sent by God to save Spain.

Catholic nuns leading Spanish children to school, 1951

Control of the press

Instrctions issued to the media following the death of Spanish writer, Ortega y Gasset: "Each newspaper may publish up to three articles on the death of Ortega y Gasset: one biographical piece and two commentaries. All articles on the writer's philosophy must emphasise his errors in religious matters. On the front page photographs of the funeral parlour, the death mask or the corpse may be published, but not photographs of Ortega during his lifetime."

In the long-term, Franco aimed to create popular enthusiasm for the new regime and for himself as leader. In this way, he would no longer need the support of the monarchists or the Falange. Propaganda presented Franco as the saviour of Spain – a **messiah** who would create a newly powerful and glorious nation. In so doing he undermined popular support for the monarchy and helped to consolidate his own position.

The Church

From the very beginning of the regime, there was an unofficial alliance between the Catholic Church and the Franco government. Republican persecution of the Church during the civil war had cemented the relationship between the Church and the Nationalists. The legal basis of this alliance was set out in the 1938 Clerical Laws, which gave the Church an important role within the New State. These laws gave the Church a monopoly over primary education in Spain. They also allowed the Church to run youth groups independent of the Falange youth movement. Finally, religions other than Christianity were outlawed, and the rights of Protestant Churches were severely restricted.

The Clerical Laws gave the Catholic Church a considerable degree of independence within Spain. Franco could afford this because he knew he could count on their support. One reason for the Church's support was that it endorsed Franco's continuing crusade against atheists and Marxists. Therefore, the Church remained silent about the atrocities committed by the regime. Consequently, while the Church did not officially support executions, its silence strongly implied that Catholics should not oppose Franco's terror tactics.

More generally, the Church supported Franco's conservative vision of society in which men governed their families, marriage was respected, and rich and poor could come together and worship God on a Sunday. The Church's support was invaluable because it persuaded Catholics, a significant proportion of Spanish society, that the New State was God's gift to Spain and deserved their support.

Censorship and propaganda

The new regime's strict **control of the press** began during the civil war. The Press Law of April 1938 meant that government authorisation was required for publications of any kind. It also gave the government the power to shut down any publication. Finally, it gave the government the right to appoint the editors of Spain's 45 daily newspapers and to sack their journalists. Publishers had no right of appeal. Even after the Nationalists' victory, the civil war played a big part in government propaganda. From 1942, the propaganda department produced short news films celebrating Franco's achievements and reminding the Spanish people of the horrors of the Red Terror. These were broadcast before every feature film and therefore reached a wide audience.

Economic policy

The Falange's desire to create a **totalitarian state** was partially realised in the economy. Franco adopted two fascist economic policies – corporatism and autarky – in an attempt to rebuild the economy after the civil war.

Corporatism

Corporatism was a policy advocated by fascists as a 'middle way' between capitalism and communism. Capitalism, they argued, favoured big business; communism, on the other hand, gave the workers what they wanted. Corporatism, they hoped, would hold these competing interests in balance and work for the national interest rather than the interest of one particular class.

In practice, corporatism passed economic power to the new government. All workers and employers were part of a government-controlled syndicate or corporation. In theory, the syndicates represented both the workers and the employers. The government used the syndicates to impose wage rates, production targets and the prices at which goods could be sold. Central Syndical Councils of Co-ordination organised the syndicates in each region, and special courts were created to arbitrate between workers and employers when disputes occurred.

Corporatism helped Franco in two ways:

- First, it helped to control the working class. It replaced independent trade unions and therefore it stopped workers organising themselves against the regime.

- Second, it won the loyalty of many Falangists who believed that the creation of a corporatist economy was the first step on the road to a fascist state.

Autarky

Autarky was also a popular policy with the Falangists. Franco argued that it would help Spain to grow and make everything the Spanish people needed. He believed that this policy would form the basis of his new imperial military state and provide for the well-being of the Spanish people. Consequently, economic controls were instituted to make it practically impossible to import or export goods. Autarky was never perfect, and a small quantity of trade continued. Nonetheless, throughout this period, Spain owed only 5% of its **gross domestic product (GDP)** to trade.

Results

Franco's economic policy between 1939 and 1945 was a success in terms of pleasing the Falange and preventing challenges to his power, but it was a disaster for the Spanish economy. Corporatism proved to be a good way of controlling powerful interest groups, but it failed to inspire economic innovation. In addition, corporatism led to a decline in the standard of living for workers as fixed wages failed to keep up with price increases. Indeed, in the 1940s, wages increased by an average of only 30%, compared to an almost 600% increase in prices.

Glossary

Totalitarian state

A form of government in which all areas of life are brought under government control. Totalitarianism is different from traditional dictatorships because it demands enthusiastic commitment from its citizens, whereas traditional dictatorships merely expect a lack of opposition. Classic examples of totalitarian states are Nazi Germany and Stalin's Russia.

Fascism and totalitarianism are often linked but they are different things. Stalin's Russia is often described as totalitarian, and yet it was a communist regime. Equally, Mussolini's Italy was a fascist regime which never became fully totalitarian.

Conservative authoritarianism is often mistaken for totalitarianism. These regimes enforce a traditional social, religious and economic order, through coercion and propaganda. Traditional sources of authority such as the Church or aristocrats tend to play a big role. These regimes do not attempt to control all aspects of life, seeking conformity rather than enthusiasm.

Autarky

Economic self-sufficiency.

Gross domestic product (GDP)

A measure of the total wealth produced by a nation in one year.

Autarky created a legion of problems.

- First, Spain made synthetic (artificial) substitutes for materials which it did not possess – for example, making oil from coal, and replacing cotton with synthetic fibres made from expensive chemicals. These synthesised materials were of low quality and were extremely expensive to produce. It would have been cheaper and more efficient to import these materials and, in this sense, autarky wasted resources.

- Second, there were some goods that were not imported and could not be synthesised. These included fertilisers. Without these, food production declined. Indeed, during the 1940s, Spain produced only a quarter of the amount of cereal each year that had been produced in 1935. As a result, 200,000 people died of malnutrition and the period became known as '*Los Años de Hambre*' – the years of hunger.

- Finally, autarky meant that the Spanish economy would never benefit from foreign investment or trade. During the 1940s, international trade played a crucial role in bringing about economic growth in Europe. Franco's policy of autarky prevented Spain from enjoying these benefits.

The Spanish economy also suffered as a result of Franco's commitment to the military. Between 1939 and 1945, around 50% of government spending was devoted to the military. As a result, investment in agriculture and industry was neglected. Agriculture was further affected by the drought of 1944–45. Although the government tried to use this disaster to its advantage, blaming it for the fall in living standards, in reality Franco's policies made the results of the drought far worse than they might have been.

Terror

Franco had no desire to make peace with those who had opposed him during the civil war. Rather, he wanted to continue the violent '**purification**' of society which had begun during it. In February 1939 he introduced the Law of Political Responsibilities. This criminalised radical political activities going back to 1934. In this sense, it allowed the New State to settle old scores from the civil war years. Indeed, much of the terror in the early years of the regime dealt with the legacy of the civil war.

The Law of Political Responsibilities operated within a new military framework, which placed the police and the Falange militia under military control. The police were tasked with arresting suspected radicals. Then the police handed the suspects over to military courts. The courts had wide-ranging powers and could sentence people to death, send them to prison, exile them or place them under house arrest. Very little evidence was needed to convict people under the new law. Around 500,000 people were convicted of breaking the law by 1945, and more than 200,000 were executed. Executions were carried out by the Falange militia.

The law targeted those who were believed to be 'un-Spanish', people who had values 'foreign' to those of the nation. The groups most likely to be affected by the law were urban workers, poor peasants, people who had campaigned for regional rights, liberated women and middle-class liberals who had supported the Republic.

Purification: The Butcher of Malaga

When Malaga fell to the Nationalists, the new State Prosecutor – Carlos Arias Navarro – instigated a purge of potential dissidents. In the period 8–14 February 1937, 3500 Spaniards were executed there by the Nationalists; between 15 February and 25 August 1944, a further 17,000 Spaniards were killed. The slaughter earned Arias Navarro the nickname 'The Butcher of Malaga'.

As well as 'purifying' Spanish society, the law helped to strengthen Franco's control. The arrests and executions led to an atmosphere of fear, in which people were unwilling to speak out against the regime. Franco's treatment of his enemies was so vicious that it shocked even Heinrich Himmler, the head of Hitler's secret police and architect of the Holocaust. The people of Spain called these dark years 'a time of silence'.

Foreign policy, 1939–56

The Second World War

Initially, Franco's foreign policy reflected the alliances that he had made during the civil war, particularly with Nazi Germany.

On 23 October 1940, Franco met Hitler to discuss Spanish entry into the war. By this time, Hitler had conquered France and Britain alone stood in the way of Germany's dominance of Europe. At the meeting, Franco said that he would enter an alliance with Germany and Italy against Britain in return for territorial gains including French territory in Morocco. However, Hitler was unwilling to agree to this. Italy, too, wanted territory in Morocco and Hitler felt that, as Franco had contributed nothing to France's defeat, he should not benefit from it. The negotiations failed, and Spain stayed neutral.

Nonetheless, in the early part of the war, Spanish neutrality favoured Hitler. Franco sent the Blue Division – 18,000 Spanish volunteers – to fight alongside the German Army from 1941. In addition, he sent raw materials to Germany, sent workers to work in German factories and allowed German submarines (U-Boats) to refuel in Spanish harbours.

At the same time, Franco was aware that the outcome of the war was uncertain and therefore did not cut his ties with the western Allies. To this end, he did a great deal to avoid directly engaging with Allied troops. For example, he sent Spanish volunteers to fight against Russia on the Eastern Front rather than sending them to the Western Front to fight against the British. Franco hoped that his neutrality would be enough to win Hitler's favour without provoking the wrath of Britain.

By 1942, Franco had become increasingly convinced that Germany would lose the war. In 1941, America had entered the war, tipping the balance in the Allies' favour. Consequently, in 1943 Franco had distanced himself from Germany and organised the withdrawal of the Blue Division from Russia.

The consequences of neutrality

In the short term, neutrality was beneficial for Franco and for Spain. The war put Franco in a difficult position as the two most powerful factions within his government disagreed on what Spain should do. The monarchists argued that Spain should side with Britain, as the Spanish monarchy had strong links to the British monarchy. The Falange, on the other hand, sided with their fellow fascists in Germany and Italy. By remaining neutral, Franco was able to keep the support of both factions and in so doing retain control of the government.

Neutrality was also beneficial for Spain. Britain and the US, for example, provided Spain with oil during the war, in return for the promise that Spain would not enter the war on Germany's side.

Take note

Taking notes is not just copying the text. Your notes should be summaries of the key points. The following method of note-taking may help you to develop this skill.

Divide a large sheet of paper in half. Write the final two 'key questions' from the beginning of the chapter on your piece of paper, one at the top of each column. Read through the next two sections of the chapter on foreign policy and social policy. Do not write anything down, but do keep in mind the two key questions. When you have finished reading, close the book. From memory, write bullet-pointed answers to the two questions. When you have finished writing from memory, read back through the section again. Try to remember any key points you may have missed the first time. Close the book and add to your notes.

Franco meets Hitler, October 1940

Glossary

United Nations (UN)

An international organisation set up in 1945 with the aim of fostering international co-operation, safeguarding human rights and preventing another war.

Marshall Plan (1948–52)

An American initiative creating a free-trade zone in Western Europe in exchange for American economic aid. The plan was designed to help Europe recover after the Second World War.

Cold War

An ideological and economic conflict between communist Russia and capitalist America, and their allies, following the Second World War. Although it is called a 'war', the two sides never directly fought each other – hence a 'cold' war.

Concordat

A formal agreement between the Catholic Church and a nation state, which recognises a special role of the Church in the life of a nation. It also implies papal approval of the government of that nation.

At the same time, Spain supplied Germany with raw materials and bought goods from Latin America on Germany's behalf. Initially, Spain received no payment for these as Spain was heavily indebted to Germany from the civil war. However, as the war progressed and Hitler became more reliant on Spain's help, Germany started to pay for Spanish aid in gold. Finally, staying out of the war allowed Spain a chance to rebuild rather than committing its resources to a new and costly war.

Foreign policy after 1945

The Cold War

Intially, Franco's regime was associated with the fascist regimes that had aided its victory in the civil war. As a result, Spain was excluded from the **United Nations** and the **Marshall Plan**. Spain's diplomatic position changed in the late 1940s due to the development of the **Cold War**. America wanted allies in the fight against communism and therefore turned to Franco, a long standing opponent of communism.

In 1949 Franco negotiated a $25 million loan from America – the first in a series of loans to Spain which would eventually total $625 million. In return, Franco allowed American troops to establish bases on Spanish territory.

Spain's position improved further during the early 1950s.

- In 1953 Franco signed the Treaty of Madrid, granting the USA the right to set up military bases on Spanish soil. By 1959 the Americans had four bases in Spain.

- In 1953 Franco also negotiated a **concordat** with the Vatican, signifying that Franco's government enjoyed the approval of the Pope. Indeed, under the terms of the concordat, Franco was given the right to appoint bishops in Spain.

- Finally, in 1955, Spain joined the UN. This paved the way for further international collaboration during the 1960s.

Social policy, 1939–56

Franco's social policy changed little from 1939 to 1956. In many ways, life in Franco's New State was a continuation of life under the Nationalists during the civil war.

Women's freedom was significantly diminished. In 1938, Franco reintroduced the 1889 Civil Code, which made women legally dependent on first their fathers and then, after marriage, their husbands. He also reintroduced sections of the 1870 Criminal Code, which meant that women could be punished in criminal courts for extra-marital affairs. Additionally, all single women aged between 18 and 35 had to undertake six months of voluntary service as part of the Falange's *Sección Femenina*, designed to prepare them for a life selflessly dedicated to the Catholic family and the nation.

In accordance with the teaching of the Church, the New State actively persecuted lesbian women, gay men and bisexuals. Gay men were the main focus of government action.

Homosexuality was only formally outlawed in 1954 but, before 1954, persecution of gay men was encouraged by the state. Men who were convicted of homosexual acts were sent to '*galerías de invertidos*' ('deviant galleries') which were supposed to 'cure' them.

The government also used propaganda to stress the importance of marriage and the family. Propaganda films were made in Spain featuring heroes and heroines who were committed to their families. Equally, government censors used their power to re-edit foreign films to take out references to extra-marital affairs. In some cases, films were simply redubbed to turn characters that were having affairs into married couples. In other cases, the film would be re-edited and scripts partially re-written. In these cases, couples who were having affairs would be turned into brothers and sisters in order to explain their closeness, and love scenes between people who were unmarried were cut.

Conclusion: Franco's Spain – in from the cold?

Between 1939 and 1956, Franco constructed a New State in which his enemies were ruthlessly oppressed by the army and the Falange, social policy was set by conservatives and the Catholic Church, and economic growth was stifled by autarky and corporatism. In the aftermath of the Second World War, the prominence of the Falange, and the conservatism of the regime, convinced many that Franco's regime was a fascist state which had no place in the international community. Nonetheless, as the Cold War developed, America and the West were prepared to overlook the oppressive elements of Franco's Spain and work together against communism.

> ### Comment from the Cardinal Primate of Spain, 1959
> "Public bathing on beaches, in swimming pools or from river banks constitutes a special danger for morality. Mixed bathing must be avoided because it almost always gives rise to sin and scandal. As for engaged couples, they must shun solitude and obscurity. Walking arm in arm is unacceptable. It is scandalous and indecent to walk about linked in any way whatsoever."

Taking it further

The historian of fascism, Roger Eatwell, argues that in a truly fascist society the government would use its power to strip the traditional elites – such as the Church, big businesses and landowners – of their power in order to create a new society based on the glory of the nation. He also argues that 'the essentially conservative' dictatorship of General Franco in Spain 'never attempted this and that therefore Franco's Spain was never truly fascist'. Using the information in this chapter, how far do you agree with the view that, between 1939 and 1956, Spain was not a fascist regime?

Taking it further

For more information on fascism and totalitarianism, the following may be useful: Roger Griffin's, *The Nature of Fascism* (1991), Leonard Schapiro's, *Totalitarianism* (1972).

Take note: revision

Read through your notes on this chapter. Highlight ten pieces of information that you think are vital to understanding this period. Use these ten pieces of information as the basis for a ten-question quiz. Write down your questions, remembering also to record the answers. Form groups of two. Take it in turns to ask your partner your ten questions. How well have they learnt the information in the chapter? Are there are any particular areas of weakness? Use their test results to set them two targets for revision. For example, if they incorrectly answered your questions about economic policy, you may decide that they need to focus on this when they revise.

Activity: Propaganda posters

Imagine you are a member of Franco's government in 1956. Create a propaganda poster advertising the achievements of the New State. Your poster will be most effective if you compare Spain in 1956 to Spain under the Second Republic.

Or

Imagine you are a Spanish Republican based in Paris in 1956. Create a propaganda poster criticising Franco's regime. Your poster will be most effective if you stress the weakness of the economy and the limitations of personal freedom within the New State.

Activity: Totalitarian control?

On a large piece of paper, draw five concentric circles. Label the circle in the centre 'Totalitarian control' and the circle on the outside 'Weak government control'.

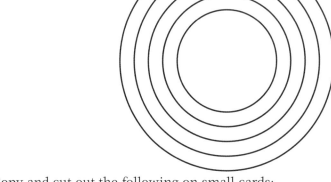

Copy and cut out the following on small cards:
- Law of Political Responsibilities
- Corporatism
- Treatment of women
- Treatment of the press
- Autarky
- Use of propaganda
- Treatment of lesbian women, gay men and bisexuals
- Foreign policy
- The Church

Re-read the definition of a totalitarian state on page 75. Now reread your notes on the topics listed on the small cards. For each card, reach a judgment about the extent to which Franco's policies reflected totalitarian control and place each card in an appropriate place on the concentric circles diagram. Cards that represent a strong degree of totalitarian control should be placed closer to the centre of the diagram, while cards that do not represent totalitarian control should be placed towards the outside. Next to each card, write a brief explanation of why you have placed it where you have.

Now use your diagram to plan an answer to the exam-style question: 'How far had Spain become a totalitarian state by 1956?'

Chapter 10: **Dictatorship transformed, 1956–75**

Key questions

- Why did the influence of the Falange decline in the late 1950s?
- In what ways did Franco's economic policy change after 1956?
- How far did Spanish society change in the period 1956–75?
- What was the impact of political reform in the 1960s?
- Why did some groups oppose Franco's regime?
- How far was Spain modernised in the period 1956–75?

The transformation of Spain that took place between 1956 and 1975 was based on the mutual exchange of sweat. Holiday-makers from Northern Europe came and sweated on Spanish beaches, while Spanish labourers moved abroad to sweat in British, French and German factories. The tourists brought liberal ideas and much-needed cash, and the Spanish labourers returned with healthy bank balances and the experience of democracy. This mutual exchange would have been unthinkable in 1955, but the economic crisis of the late 1950s acted as a catalyst for reform.

Timeline

February 1957	Cabinet reshuffle demoted Falange ministers and promoted Opus Dei
May 1958	New Principles of the Movement published
June–July 1959	Stabilisation Plan; ETA founded
1962	Spain's application to join the EEC rejected; Strikes in Asturias
December 1964	Law of Associations
April 1965	SEU dissolved
March 1966	Press Act
1967	Organic Law; Law on Family Representation; Religious Freedom Act
August 1968	ETA assassinated the Head of the Political Section of the Police in Guipuzcoa
1969	'Concordat Jail' set up in Zamora
April 1970	Falange renamed the National Movement
February 1973	*The Church and the Political Community* published

Take note

Earlier you read about Franco's economic policy in the period 1939–45. Before you read the next four sections, make a list of the key features of that policy. As you read through these sections, note down the ways in which this policy changed in the period 1956–75.

The economy

Economic crisis

Between 1956 and 1959, Spain endured its biggest crisis since the civil war. The price of goods was increasing by as much as 20% in a year, far faster than wages or production, and this forced a change in economic policy.

This policy change had two important consequences:

- It swept away one of the most powerful factions within the Spanish elite.
- It led to a social transformation.

Glossary

Inflation

A period when the value of money decreases and prices increase.

Opus Dei

A Catholic organisation founded in 1928. In Franco's Spain, Catholic groups were able to organise themselves independently in a way that political parties and trade unions were not. Consequently, Opus Dei became a centre for people with a specific vision for society. The organisation was made up of highly qualified and highly educated people, often with professional jobs or teaching posts in the universities. At the time, Opus Dei rejected democracy and believed that human equality was a dangerous myth. They were committed to the high moral standards preached by the Church.

Economic crisis and the fall of the Falange

The transformation in Spain's diplomatic position in the 1950s triggered an economic crisis. Following the Treaty of Madrid, Spain received American loans and investment. However, the Spanish government continued to discourage international trade and, consequently, the loans could only be spent within Spain. As a result, there was more currency in circulation, decreasing its value. This was reflected in the increase in prices – an economic problem known as **inflation**.

These economic troubles led to a political crisis. Students and workers protested, demanding better living conditions and political reform. Jose Arrese, a leading Falangist, argued that the crisis could only be solved by turning Spain into a fully fascist state. The Arrese Plan advised a return to strict autarky and the strengthening of national syndicalism. However, Franco rejected the plan and used the crisis as an opportunity to turn against the Falangists.

By the late 1950s, the Falange had become an embarrassment. Franco wanted to make alliances with Western democracies. However, Franco's association with the apparently fascist Falange made this process difficult. Equally, the Falange could no longer claim to be a dynamic mass movement. An official report showed that the Falange had not grown in number since 1942. Unofficially, Franco was informed that active membership had declined sharply. Evidently, Franco could sideline the Falange without becoming unpopular. Therefore, in the cabinet reshuffle of 1957, the remaining members of the Falange were demoted, given low-ranking jobs such as Ministers of Labour, Education and Housing.

As the Falange declined, Franco promoted a new group of politicians associated with **Opus Dei**. In contrast to the Falange, members of Opus Dei were given high-ranking positions such as director of the *Banco Popular* and Minister of Trade, which gave them control of the economy. In this way, Franco used Opus Dei to replace the Falange at the top levels of government.

By 1970 the marginalisation of the Falange was complete. On 3 April, a new law was passed which changed the name of the movement. The name Falange was dropped and the party was rebranded the National Movement. The name change severed the link between the party and its radical fascist past, and symbolised the Falange's final decline.

The technocrats and the free market

The rise of Opus Dei in 1957 led to a radical shift in the regime's economic policy. The change was significant because it marked the decisive break between Franco's New State and the Falange. From this point on, the fascist aspects of the regime disappeared and the capitalist and Catholic aspects of the regime came to the forefront.

Franco's new elite were economic experts. They were known as technocrats. That is to say, they were promoted to high office due to their technical expertise. The technocrats believed that the most effective way to solve the financial crisis was to allow greater economic freedom and remove government control of the economy. This change in direction was reflected in the publication of a new set of principles for Franco's government, which no longer described Spain as a 'National Syndicalist State'. Instead, capitalism was restored and the **free market** began to operate.

The new policy was set out in the 1959 Stabilisation Plan which aimed to solve Spain's economic problems by increasing international trade, cutting public spending and allowing the price of goods such as petrol and tobacco, and services such as transportation, to increase to their market levels. The promotion of trade signalled the end of autarky, while the change to pricing weakened the power of the corporations, which had previously controlled price levels.

Glossary

Free market

An economic term which describes a specific type of economic system. In a free market, citizens are free to compete against each other as purchasers and providers of goods and services. The government plays an extremely limited role and therefore production, consumption and prices are determined by the needs of the consumer.

Economic miracle

Between 1960 and 1975, Spain's economy was transformed, becoming one of the fastest-growing economies in the world. During this period, Franco claimed that his policy of *desarrollismo* (developmentism) was responsible for Spain's economic miracle. However, recent historians have questioned this and suggested that Spain's prosperity had more to do with the willingness of foreign countries to invest in Spain.

In practice, *desarrollismo* took the form of a series of development plans. They followed the emphasis on the free market which had been introduced in the Stabilisation Plan of 1959.

Spain's economic boom, or *despegue* (take-off), was based on four factors:

- the free-market policies of the technocrats
- foreign investment
- emigration
- tourism.

The free-market policies of the technocrats included the ending of autarky. This, in turn, opened Spain up to foreign investment, particularly from America and Western Europe, where economies were growing strongly. Ending autarky also allowed Spanish labourers to seek work abroad, and encouraged tourism within Spain.

Between 1960 and 1974, the Spanish economy attracted $7.6 billion of **foreign investment**, and more than $1 billion in loans. Around 40% of this investment came from the USA. Germany and Britain also invested heavily, accounting for around 20% of the investment between them. Foreign investment helped to modernise the Spanish economy by encouraging the production of high-tech goods. For example, by 1970, 50% of investment in the Spanish car industry, 42% of investment in electronics and 37% of investment in the chemical industry came from overseas.

Foreign investment in Spain, 1959–73

Year	Amount (million pesetas)
1959	3,895
1960	7,012
1961	10,285
1962	7,534
1963	14,258
1964	17,023
1965	20,285
1966	25,056
1967	34,341
1968	38,430
1969	43,425
1970	60,954
1971	65,362
1972	85,249
1973	105,430

The decision to open Spain's borders and allow a free market of labour also helped the economic boom.

- From 1959, Spanish workers started to emigrate, seeking work in the advanced economies of north-west Europe. This drastically reduced Spanish unemployment. What is more, Spaniards who worked abroad tended to send some of their wages home. In 1959, 500,000 Spaniards emigrated, sending around $126 million back to Spain. In the next decade, a further one million Spaniards went to work abroad. Consequently, unemployment remained low.

- Spain opened its borders to tourists, and the wealth they brought with them. In 1959, over four million tourists came to Spain to enjoy the good weather and sun-soaked beaches, bringing in $128 million. By 1965 the figure had leapt to over 14 million, pumping over $1 billion dollars into the Spanish economy. A decade later, 30 million tourists would spend almost $3.5 billion on holiday in Spain.

In this way, the economic boom was largely due to tourism and foreign investment. However, the technocrats deserve some credit for the achievement – they opened up the economy and in so doing allowed Spain to benefit from an influx of foreign money.

Consumer boom

The economic boom led to the creation of a consumer economy (see table).

	1960	1975
Percentage of households with refrigerators	4	87
Percentage of households with televisions	1	89
Average calories consumed per day	2116	2968
Amount of protein consumed per day (grams)	64	92

The consumer boom was linked to an increase in leisure time on the part of Spanish workers. The decline in unemployment meant that employers had a smaller labour market from which to choose workers. This gave workers greater bargaining power over working conditions. Consequently, Spanish workers were able to demand shorter working weeks: on average, male citizens worked 49 hours a week in the late 1960s; this had fallen to 44 hours by 1975.

The limits of prosperity

The economic boom did not benefit all equally. By 1970, Spain's richest 1% owned 22% of the country's wealth, whereas the poorest 52% of the population owned just over 20% of the country's wealth. Indeed, economic inequality was worse than in other European countries such as Britain, where the richest 1% owned approximately 11% of the nation's wealth.

House building also failed to keep pace with demand in urban areas. The problem was so bad in Barcelona in the early 1960s that a **shanty town** – or *chabola* – housing 70,000 people developed on Montjuic, a hill near the centre of the city. Government housing projects were also inadequate.

In Madrid – another city with a profound housing shortage – there were 50,000 unoccupied luxury flats which the relatively poor workers could not afford to rent.

Tourism was also a mixed blessing. By 1965, 53% of government investment in roads was allocated to towns with holiday resorts. However, only 30% of the Spanish population lived in these areas. By contrast, inland Spain, home to 48% of the population, received only 12% of investment in roads. In this sense, tourists benefited much more from government investment than the people of Spain themselves.

The Spanish regions did not gain equally from modernisation. Average personal income in the Balearic Islands, a hot spot for tourists, was more than double that in rural areas such as Andalusia and Extremadura. Poverty was still widespread in these regions, and the average income of farmers was only 40% of the average income across Europe as a whole.

Social change

The impact of the economic boom

The economic boom led to important social changes. First, Spanish society was transformed in terms of social class. New, relatively well-paid jobs in industry and tourism attracted agricultural workers, who left the countryside to work in the cities and new resorts. In 1940, Spain was a predominantly agricultural country, with the majority of people working the land. By 1975, only 22% of Spanish people worked in agriculture. Around 38% of the population worked in industry and the remaining 40% worked in tourism.

Education also benefited from the economic boom. During the 1960s, the government, for the first time, spent more on education than it did on the military. Infant schools were open in all but the most remote of Spanish villages and, as a result, illiteracy declined from 11% in 1960 to 6% in 1970. The government invested in universities too. The number of universities in Spain shot up from 12 in 1959 to 22 in 1974. In the same period, the number of students going to university increased by 500% and the number of women attending university increased – by 1970, approximately one third of university students were female.

Social welfare improved as well. By 1974, 79% of working people were covered by the government's social welfare schemes, compared to 29% in 1950. Similarly, healthcare improved. There was a considerable increase in the number of doctors practising in Spain. In 1950 there was one doctor to every 650 citizens; by 1975, there was a doctor for every 106 citizens. As a result, infant mortality declined from around 43 deaths per 1000 births in 1960 to around 28 in 1970. Additionally, life expectancy increased, from around 62 years in 1950 to 73 years in 1975.

The next three sections detail the impact of three forces on Spanish society:
- the economic boom
- tourism
- the Catholic Church.

Make bullet-pointed notes on the impact of these forces.
- Decide whether each force modernised Spain or kept Spain wedded to traditional values, and to what extent it did this.
- Decide how many people were affected by this force.

Write a paragraph in answer to the question: 'To what extent was Spanish society modernised in the period 1956–75?'

Furthermore, the new consumer economy brought about additional social change. New advertising promoted an untraditional, pleasure-seeking lifestyle. Advertising endorsed youth fashions such as riding motor scooters, drinking, dating, pop music and long hair for men. Youth culture influenced spending habits and, by 1971, 56% of teenagers owned a record player and 82% owned a radio. Smoking was promoted as fashionable in films and in advertising. By 1971, 63% of men and 44% of women smoked, usually preferring American-style cigarettes. Cinema attendance increased rapidly. Indeed, Spain had the second-highest cinema attendance in the world. The dating culture was also used to advertise products. For example, an advert for toothpaste featured a young woman who told her boyfriend, 'Pepe, I love you, but if you use Colgate I shall love you more.'

In sum, economic modernisation initiated the most important social changes in Spanish history. By 1975, Spain was a predominantly urban country, its citizens better educated, healthier and more Western than ever before.

The impact of tourism

Tourism also brought about social change in Spain. The impact of tourism was twofold.

- On the one hand, Spain was influenced by the modern Western values which tourists brought with them to Spain.

- On the other hand, Spain was forced to change in order to keep its share of the tourist market.

Initially, there was an element of culture shock when tourists from France, Germany and Britain arrived in Spain. Conservative Spanish Catholics were shocked by the revealing nature of the bikinis being worn on their beaches. In the words of one priest, modern swimwear turned women into tempting 'carnal goddesses'. As a result, while bikinis were permitted on the beach, they were banned in Spanish towns. The government even constructed 'dressing houses' along the coast to allow women to dress properly before leaving the beach. However, fear of losing the lucrative tourist trade meant that these restrictions were rarely enforced, and by the early 1960s the bikini was widely tolerated. Indeed, where the tourists led, locals followed, and many Spaniards imitated foreign fashion, with Spanish women wearing bikinis and men wearing shorts.

Setting aside the bikini, tourism led to the adoption of liberal Western values more generally. Many more women entered the work force as tour guides and maids in hotels. Indeed, the number of women in the work force shot up from only 16% in 1950 to 30% in 1974. The Spanish tourist industry was also keen to cast off the traditional image of Spain as a conservative Catholic country. Rather, it went along with the image of 'sand, sun and sex' that promoted package holidays to Spain during the 1970s.

Cover of a Thomas Cook holiday brochure, 1964

The limits of social change

In spite of these changes, the 1960s and 1970s did not see the complete destruction of Spanish tradition. Indeed, the moral teachings of the Church continued to have a powerful hold over social policy, particularly in the area of women's rights and sexual morality. The Catholic Church had a strong influence on the school curriculum and therefore sex education stressed the need to abstain from sex before marriage. In accordance with the teaching of the Church, the production and sale of pornography was prohibited by law, artificial forms of contraception such as condoms and the contraceptive pill were banned, abortion was illegal and homosexuality remained unlawful. These measures were quite effective – indeed, a study published in 1973 showed that 86% of women who described themselves as Catholic did not use any form of contraception. Equally, government reports show that Spanish women who were able to get hold of condoms illegally had difficulty persuading their partners to use them.

The Catholic moral code was reinforced in the media. Spanish romantic comedies often contrasted promiscuous female tourists with virtuous Spanish women. Significantly, the Spanish women always got the man in the end. What is more, popular television programmes mocked homosexual men.

However, Catholic morality did not wholly prevent the practices that they condemned. There was a black market in pornography and contraception. Dangerous back-street abortions were prevalent – the government estimated that approximately 300,000 were conducted in 1974 alone, resulting in the deaths of 3000 women – while wealthy Spanish women could fly to other European countries and have an abortion in the safety of a properly equipped hospital.

Political reform

Spain's dependence on foreign investment and tourism forced a limited degree of political reform during the 1960s. In much of Europe, Spain was still viewed as a dictatorship and, as a result, Spain's 1962 application to join the **European Economic Community** was rejected. Manuel Fraga, Minister for Information and Tourism, was concerned that this rejection would discourage tourism. As a result, he championed a series of measures which allowed him to claim that Spain was becoming a more liberal country.

First, in 1964, the Spanish government introduced the Law of Associations. This legalised the formation of small groups as long as they were not political in nature. Prior to the law, the only groups that were officially recognised were part of the Falange. Following the law, there was an explosion in community activity, particularly amongst women, who formed housewives' federations, parent groups and neighbourhood associations. Later in the 1960s, many of these cultural groups became centres of resistance to the Franco regime.

Take note

Draw a table to compare the following in the period 1956–64 with the period 1964–75: social organisations, press censorship, political structure and the role of the Church. Use the notes you made earlier to complete the column on 1956–64. Complete the final column using the information in the following section. Add a third column to discuss the impact any changes had on the regime and the Spanish people, and complete this as you work through the section.

Glossary

European Economic Community (EEC)

An international organisation created in 1957 to promote trade among key European countries. Initially, the members included Belgium, France, Germany, Italy, Luxembourg and the Netherlands. In 1993, it was renamed the European Union (EU).

Secondly, the 1966 Press Act repealed earlier censorship measures. It allowed newspaper owners to appoint their own editorial teams. Additionally, newspaper stories were no longer censored prior to publication. Rather, journalists were legally free as long as they showed 'respect for truth and morality and obedience to the principles of the National Movement'. On occasions where the government felt that newspaper stories had overstepped the mark, fines were imposed and editors could be suspended, or – for repeated offences – sacked. The Press Act was significant because it allowed much greater journalistic freedom, which gradually undermined the authority of Franco's government. In addition, it was a symbolic step away from dictatorship.

Thirdly, Franco presented the Organic Law of January 1967 – in his words, a 'broad democratisation of political process'. In theory, this law introduced some aspects of the **separation of powers**, specifically creating the role of Prime Minister in addition to that of President. However, in practice, Franco occupied the role of President and Prime Minister and therefore the Organic Law did not significantly affect his power. The law also created more elected representatives in the Cortes, though these formed only 20% of the entire membership of the parliament, and political parties remained illegal. The Law on Family Representation of the same year allowed the heads of families – that is to say men and women who were married – to vote. In so doing, it extended voting rights to some women.

Finally, in July 1967, the Religious Freedom Act was introduced. The act decriminalised the practice of non-Christian religions in Spain, and permitted civil marriages – marriages that did not involve a church service. Nonetheless, there were still restrictions on the public practice of other religions. The Catholic Church was critical of the law because it threatened its position within Spanish society. The most obvious sign that the act had been passed was the opening of a synagogue in Madrid in 1968.

Opposition

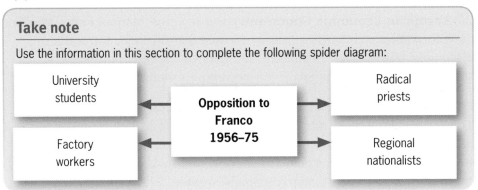

> **Take note**
>
> Use the information in this section to complete the following spider diagram:
>
> University students ← **Opposition to Franco 1956–75** → Radical priests
>
> Factory workers ← **Opposition to Franco 1956–75** → Regional nationalists

As the economy boomed and politics liberalised, opposition to the regime increased from people who felt that reform had not gone far enough, and that the economic boom was creating new problems.

Glossary

Separation of powers

A system of government in which different branches of government have separate roles. It is designed to stop one person becoming all-powerful.

Opposition came from four main sources:

- university students
- factory workers
- radical priests
- regional nationalists.

Student protests against the regime and in favour of democracy came to a head in 1964 and 1965. Students marched, went on strike and occupied buildings. As a result, university education was permanently disrupted during the late 1960s and early 1970s. The authorities responded in 1965 by banning the official Student Union (SEU), but they also instructed the police to deal with the protests cautiously. The students viewed this as weakness on the part of the government and as a result protests continued.

Student demands changed over time. In the 1960s students called for democracy, in the 1970s students radicalised. Anarchism became fashionable again and students attacked capitalism as well as Franco's dictatorship. In 1969 the government announced that it wanted to win over student radicals by encouraging them to join the National Movement. However, the initiative failed as traditional Catholic moral teaching and free-market capitalism proved unappealing to the students. As a result, the government resorted to repression. In Granada, for example, student unrest led to the implementation of martial law during the winter of 1971. In the same year, the police identified a number of radical university lecturers in Caceres who were subsequently sacked. The repression failed to stop the protests.

Workers' unrest took the form of strikes. There was a growing trend towards **strike action** from the late 1960s onwards. The strikes tended to focus on economic goals, such as better pay and conditions, rather than demands for political reform. The first big wave of unofficial strikes took place in 1962 in Asturias, the Basque Country and Barcelona. Workers organised illegal Workers' Commissions in protest at low pay. Solis Ruiz, head of the **Syndical Organisation**, personally spoke to the strike's leaders to try and negotiate a compromise. In the late 1960s illegal strikes of this type became a regular feature of Spanish life. The biggest strikes took place in 1968 when it is estimated that 1,114,000 workers walked out, again in protest at low pay.

The growing strength of the workers' organisations was partially due to co-operation between Marxist radicals and radical Catholics who were committed to fighting for social justice. The authorities tasked the Syndical Organisation with rooting out militant workers. Indeed, following the unprecedented scale of strikes in 1974, more than 4379 workers were sacked for their militancy. The police also dealt with workers when they took their protests to the streets. On one occasion in Granada, in June 1969, police officers charged a workers' demonstration, killing three strikers. However, these measures failed to stop growing industrial unrest.

Even more worrying was the radicalisation of the Catholic clergy.

Hours lost in strikes, 1967–74

Year	Hours lost
1967	2,456,100
1968	2,224,100
1969	5,549,200
1970	6,950,900
1971	8,186,500
1972	7,469,400
1973	11,120,251
1974	18,188,895

Glossary

Syndical Organisation

The organisation tasked with overseeing corporatism within Spain.

Glossary

Basque Homeland and Freedom (ETA)

ETA is a Basque nationalist organisation. They were founded in 1959 to promote traditional Basque culture and demanded independence for the Basque region. They are an armed group widely regarded as 'terrorists'.

Traditionally, the Church had supported the regime. However, the growing inequalities and problems of free-market Spain led many young priests to question the regime's direction. In university towns it was common for 'progressive priests' to work with students; in urban areas they collaborated with workers and in the Basque region they preached sermons encouraging local nationalism. Significantly, the Concordat gave Catholic priests special legal protection and therefore it was difficult for the regime to deal with them. Nonetheless, some senior bishops were unhappy about the 'red clergy' and therefore in 1969 the regime set up the 'Concordat Jail' in Zamora, which housed the most troublesome radicals. The government also began to wage a propaganda war against the 'Marxistisation' of the Church and, in 1973, Franco wrote a letter to the Pope asking for his intervention to discipline radical priests. But it was too late to stop the spread of radical ideas – later that year the Spanish Church published *The Church and the Political Community,* publicly calling for the democratisation of Spain.

The most prominent regional opposition came from the Basque Country. The **Basque Homeland and Freedom (ETA)** launched a terrorist campaign against Spanish control in the late 1960s. Initially, ETA was engaged in a series of bank robberies. This won the group a lot of support, and they were likened to Robin Hood and his merry men – stealing from the rich to help the poor. In 1968 their campaign escalated with the assassination of the head of the political section of the police in Guipuzcoa, a Basque province. The government responded by arresting 2000 members of ETA over the next year. The same year, ETA conducted two more political assassinations and in 1970 the government uncovered a plan to assassinate Franco himself. As a result, the government organised a public military trial of ETA's leaders.

Taking it further

Following 1956, Spain's economic policy took the form of a series of plans. However, there are good reasons to believe that Franco's policies as a whole did not reflect a coherent plan.
Use your notes from the past two chapters to consider how far you agree with the statement that, in the period 1939–75, Franco's government was characterised more by improvisation than it was by planning.

The trial, which took place in Burgos in December 1970, was designed to persuade the public that ETA was a ruthless criminal organisation. However, the event backfired, and the ETA defendants used the trial to denounce Franco's regime. In the process, public support for ETA grew. Indeed, ETA won the support of many radical students who protested against their imprisonment. The ETA leaders were sentenced to death, but after international pressure this sentence was reduced to life imprisonment. ETA continued its campaign, killing 48 people before Franco's death in 1975.

Conclusion: How far was Spain transformed in this period?

Between 1956 and 1975, Spain changed dramatically. The economy was liberalised, attitudes to personal morality modernised, and politics reformed. Nonetheless, the transformation was not complete. Economic progress was patchy, and many Spaniards were still living in poverty. Moral attitudes varied according to where people lived, how old they were, and the influence of the Catholic Church. Finally, political reform had still not brought about democracy in Spain.

Activity: Happy or sad?

In pairs, make copies of the cards on the right. You will need two copies of the cards. Make one set blue and one set yellow.

Draw two lines across a large sheet of paper. Label the lines '1956' and '1974'. Label the far left-hand side of the piece of paper 'sad' and the far right-hand side 'happy'.

Re-read your notes on Spain in 1956. Consider how the situation in Spain may have affected the characters on your cards. Take your blue set and place them along the line labelled '1956', making a decision about how 'happy' or 'sad' each character might be. Write a sentence next to each card explaining your placement.

Now repeat the task for 1974. This time read your notes from this chapter and use the yellow set of cards.

Use your diagram to answer the following questions:

- Which groups of people benefited most from the transformation of Spain between 1956 and 1975?
- Which groups of people experienced the least benefit?

How far did Franco's policies in the period 1956–75 improve life for the citizens of Spain?

Hotel manager	Basque nationalist
Industrial worker	Young Catholic priest
Member of the Falange	Teenager
Female student	Business manager
Old Catholic bishop	Peasant
Member of Opus Dei	Married woman

Activity: The International Symposium on Power

You have been invited to participate in the International Symposium (an academic conference) on Power in Franco's Spain. You have been asked to present a paper (an academic lecture) on one method used by Franco to retain power in the period 1939–75.

In small groups, you must prepare a short paper on one of the following:

- use of terror
- economic reform
- political reform
- political manipulation (playing off the different factions within the government)
- support of the Church.

The symposium rules state that your paper must be structured in the following way, including:

- a short introduction, explaining the key features of the topic that you are presenting and specifying the ways in which this factor helped Franco to retain power
- three specific examples – you must explain how each example illustrates the general points made in your introduction
- a conclusion, explaining the extent to which this factor helped Franco to retain power.

Use your notes from the symposium to plan an answer to the question: 'How far did Franco use terror to maintain control in Spain in the period 1939–75?'

Taking it further

You may wish to make a PowerPoint presentation to accompany your paper. As you are presenting, your audience should make a record of your research – it may prove useful to them in the future. They should use the following headings to record your key points and examples: Title of paper; Key points from the introduction; Example 1; Example 2; Example 3. How far did the factor help Franco to maintain power in Spain?

Chapter 11: **The transition to monarchy, 1968–75**

Key questions

- Why was the transfer of power from Franco to Juan Carlos difficult?
- What steps were taken by Franco's government to overcome these problems and ensure a peaceful succession?
- How important a role did Juan Carlos himself play in the transition to 1975?
- Why did Franco's regime last so long?

Franco dominated Spanish politics for almost 40 years. Throughout this period, he underwent a series of image changes. Initially, he was the war hero, then the saviour of Spain, but in his final years he had to settle for being portrayed as Spain's favourite granddad. However, Franco was not a typical grandfather. Even in his final years, he was willing to execute his enemies and make ruthless political deals to sustain his power.

Franco's final years were dogged by ill health, renewed opposition and economic difficulties. Against this troubled background, which included the assassination of the Prime Minister, Franco and his government struggled to manage the transition from dictatorship to monarchy.

Prince Juan Carlos and Franco

Timeline	
June 1947	Law of Leadership Succession
July 1969	Franco named Juan Carlos as his successor
June 1973	Carrero Blanco appointed Prime Minister
December 1973	Carrero Blanco assassinated by ETA; Carlos Arias Navarro appointed Prime Minister
March 1974	Salvador Puig Antich executed
November 1975	Franco died

Take note

Get into pairs. Nominate one of you to be the reader and one to be the listener. The reader should read aloud one paragraph at a time from the first two sections of this chapter: The listener should listen carefully and knock on the table when one of the following factors is mentioned:

- reasons why the transfer of power from Franco to Juan Carlos was so difficult
- steps taken by Franco's government to overcome these problems and ensure a peaceful transition
- actions by Juan Carlos to support the transfer.

They should knock with their left hand when the paragraph includes a reason why the transfer of power was so difficult, with their right when it includes a step taken by Franco's government to overcome these problems and ensure a peaceful transition, and they should clap both hands together when it includes an action taken by Juan Carlos that supported the transfer.

Make sure that you note down the factors identified in three lists.

Every time the listener correctly identifies a relevant factor, and knocks with the correct hand, they receive 1 point. Every time the reader spots a factor that the listener has missed, or the listener knocks with the wrong hand, the reader gets 1 point.

After every paragraph, the reader and listener should swap roles. The person with the most points wins!

The problem of the succession

Naming an heir

By the late 1960s the issue of **succession** was becoming urgent. According to official reports, Franco was as fit as ever, but for members of the government there was no disguising Franco's physical decline. Now in his late seventies, Franco was known to fall asleep during cabinet meetings, he could no longer stand for prolonged periods (which made public appearances difficult), and he had developed a fungal infection in his mouth which made breathing difficult and required extensive surgery.

Franco's ill health was politically dangerous. Senior ministers feared that, without a clear heir, Franco's death would lead to faction fighting at the top of government, protests on the streets, and even the end of the regime. In order to avoid a political crisis, senior ministers urged Franco to formally announce his heir. As a result of this pressure, Franco finally delivered on his promise to restore the monarchy. In 1969 Franco officially proclaimed **Juan Carlos** Prince of Spain and heir to the Spanish throne.

The difficult path to succession

According to the 1947 Law of Leadership Succession, Franco had every right to appoint a successor. However, his appointment was controversial. Franco's cabinet was split between the conservatives (who were known as the '**bunker**' faction or the 'immobilists') and the reformers. The reformers welcomed Franco's decision. Juan Carlos had spoken about the need to modernise Spain, and the reformers, or *juancarlistas* as they were known, hoped that once Franco was dead Juan Carlos would lead Spain to a more democratic future. The conservatives thought that democratic reform would be a mistake. They believed that their policies had been validated by Spain's economic miracle and that democracy was dangerous and unnecessary.

Initially, the reformers seemed to have the upper hand. Juan Carlos had the backing of the American government, Franco's most influential foreign ally. In addition, Adolfo Suarez, a high-profile *juancarlista*, was able to use his position as head of Spanish television to start a campaign promoting the new prince.

However, the television campaign was not wholly successful. The campaign could not focus on Juan Carlos' desire to modernise Spain as to do so would be to undermine Franco's dictatorship. Consequently, his media image focused on his prowess as a yachtsman and his skill at judo. Furthermore, many felt that Juan Carlos was not really Spanish. He was blond and spoke with an English accent, and in both ways he did not fulfil Spanish expectations of a new king. For these reasons, the campaign backfired, and in the early seventies Juan Carlos was the subject of numerous jokes which emphasised that he was unqualified to lead the country.

Glossary

Succession
The process by which power is passed from one leader to another.

Bunker
The word bunker was a reference to Hitler's bunker, a heavily fortified underground shelter from which Hitler governed Germany in the final weeks of the Second World War. The term was used metaphorically to indicate that the 'bunker' faction were extremely defensive and had deliberately cut themselves off from the outside world.

Biography

Juan Carlos
1938–present
Juan Carlos is the grandson of Alfonso XIII, Spain's king prior to the creation of the Second Republic. Juan Carlos' parents moved to Italy when the Republic was announced, and it was there that Juan Carlos was born. In 1947, when Franco proclaimed that Spain was once again a monarchy, it was clear that Juan Carlos was Franco's preferred candidate to be future king. As a result, Juan Carlos moved back to Spain in 1948, and served in the Spanish Army during the 1950s. Juan Carlos was sometimes seen as 'Franco's puppet', but as king he led Spain towards democracy.

In 1972 the conservatives found an alternative candidate. Franco's eldest granddaughter, Doña Carmen, married Alfonso de Borbón-Dampierre, another grandson of Alfonso XIII, Spain's last king. Borbón-Dampierre was tall, dark and looked much more like a stereotypical Spanish royal than Juan Carlos. Conservatives argued that Borbón-Dampierre would be a much better king than Juan Carlos for several reasons.

- First, he had never spoken in favour of democracy and, therefore, would not destabilise the regime with poorly thought through reforms.

- Second, he was married to Franco's granddaughter and, in this sense, there would be an obvious link between Franco's government and the new regime.

- Finally, they argued that Borbón-Dampierre's **claim to the throne** was superior to that of Juan Carlos.

Two princes

Doña Carmen played an important part in Borbón-Dampierre's campaign to be recognised as Spain's next ruler. As Franco became increasingly ill, he relied on his granddaughter more and more. She used her influence to persuade Franco that Borbón-Dampierre should be given the title 'His Royal Highness' and recognised as a Spanish prince. Franco agreed to the former request, but Juan Carlos refused Borbón-Dampierre the title of prince. Rather, he gave him the title of Duke of Cadiz.

The question of the succession looked like it was settled in 1973 when Franco decided that he was no longer strong enough to run the government. He remained head of state, but appointed **Luis Carrero Blanco** as Prime Minister. Carrero Blanco appointed a new Cabinet, demoting Opus Dei conservatives. Consequently, Juan Carlos, rather than his rival, gained the support of the Cabinet.

The assassination of Carrero Blanco

Carrero Blanco's appointment as Prime Minister seemed to assure a smooth succession. On Franco's death, Carrero Blanco would continue to lead the government while Juan Carlos would take over as head of state. In this sense there was now a clear plan for the future and the regime seemed secure.

ETA, recognised this and, in an attempt to destabilise the regime, came up with 'Operation Ogre' – a daring plan to assassinate the new Prime Minister. Carrero Blanco was a committed Catholic and attended Mass every day at the same church. ETA rented a small basement flat close to the church and, over the course of ten days, dug a tunnel under the street leading to the church. On 20 December 1973, they placed 100 kg of explosives in the tunnel. As the Prime Minister drove by, the explosives were detonated. The power of the explosion was so huge that it catapulted the car over a monastery, killing Carrero Blanco.

Franco's final decision

The assassination meant that Franco's last major task as head of state was to appoint a new Prime Minister. Carrero Blanco's replacement would have the tough job of managing the succession and dealing with Spain's new crisis. In October 1973 **OPEC** had increased the price of oil by 70%. This led to an economic 'oil price shock' as Western economies started to shrink in response to the price hike. The impact on Spain was massive. European and American investment in Spain dried up, and so did tourism. Inflation started to rise, reaching 24% in 1974, and workers responded with a series of strikes. The economy went into **recession**.

In response to the terrorist attack, Franco appointed Carlos Arias Navarro (see page 76), a conservative, as the new Prime Minister. Franco chose a conservative in order to suppress the mounting opposition. Arias Navarro ordered a crackdown on ETA and working-class groups in the Spanish regions. The crackdown was spearheaded by the police, aided by new fascist groups such as *Fuerza Nueva* (The New Force) and *Guerrilleros de Cristo* (Warriors of Christ the King). The climax of the campaign was the execution of Salvador Puig Antich, an anarchist who had killed a policeman. The execution provoked an international outcry, particularly as the Spanish authorities used a cruel technique: the **garrote vil**.

ETA's campaign of violence, Spain's economic difficulties and the heavy-handed repression carried out by Arias Navarro's government, led to a resurgence of left-wing opposition and renewed street fighting between left-wing workers and the new fascist street fighters. The careful plans for an orderly succession had failed, and Franco's final year was one of the most violent of the regime.

The role of Juan Carlos

Prince of Spain, 1969–74

As Franco's heir, Juan Carlos had the following duties:

- He was required to attend ceremonial occasions such as Franco's birthday celebrations.

- He was involved in diplomacy, meeting the President of the EEC in 1969 and visiting America in 1971 for discussions with President Nixon.

- He distributed official titles amongst the Spanish royal family, such as giving Borbón-Dampierre the title Duke of Cadiz.

In practice, Juan Carlos had very little power within Spain. His role was mainly symbolic, and he had to defer to Franco on all matters with the exception of distributing titles within the royal family. However, as a diplomat he had more freedom, and when visiting other countries he could talk freely about his intentions for Spain's future.

Nonetheless, Juan Carlos was important as he was a symbol of hope. Many Spaniards believed that, after Franco's death, Juan Carlos would lead Spain to democracy.

Glossary

OPEC

OPEC (Organisation of the Petroleum Exporting Countries) is an international organisation founded in 1960. Its main purpose is to co-ordinate the oil production and distribution of several major oil-producing countries such as Iran, Iraq, Saudi Arabia and the United Arab Emirates. During 1973, OPEC used its power to dramatically increase the price of oil and in so doing created a global economic crisis.

Recession

An economic term which describes a period of six months or more in which the amount of money in an economy decreases. Recessions are usually associated with rising unemployment, rising inflation and business failures.

Garrote vil

The garrote vil is a particularly inhumane method of execution. It involves the victim's ankles, knees, waist, wrists and shoulders being tied to a chair. At the same time, a metal band is placed around the victim's neck. This band is progressively tightened, by turning a handle or a wheel, until the victim is either suffocated or their neck is snapped. In some cases a metal spike or blade is placed at the base of the neck in order to break the neck more quickly. The technique was used until 1974.

The coronation of Juan Carlos in 1975

Acting head of state

Franco was hospitalised repeatedly during 1975. During these periods Juan Carlos became temporary head of state. Yet Franco was still very much in control and continued to support Arias Navarro's repressive policies. Franco suffered a great deal in his last weeks due to the presence of blood clots in his legs. He died on 20 November 1975 at the age of 82, his last recorded words were: 'Lord, how difficult it is to die.'

Juan Carlos' coronation

Few foreign leaders attended Franco's funeral. Those who did, such as Augusto Pinochet of Chile, were themselves dictators. The coronation of Juan Carlos was quite different. The presidents of France and Germany and the Duke of Edinburgh all attended. In so doing, the international community distanced itself from the dictator and threw their weight behind the reforming king.

In 1976, less than a year after becoming king, Juan Carlos announced his intention to begin the immediate transition to democracy. The path to democracy was not easy. Conservatives tried to slow the pace of change and hindered attempts to liberalise Spain. Nonetheless, in 1982 Spain held its first general election since 1936, which, just like the last democratic election, resulted in a Socialist government.

Take note

As you read through this section, complete the following table:

Reason why Franco's regime lasted so long	Specific examples	Period when this was important	How did this factor help Franco's regime to last for so long?
Pragmatism			
Political manipulation			
Repression			
Propaganda			
Economic miracle			
Support of the elites			
Weakness of opposition			

Why did Franco's regime last so long?

Franco made his last public appearance at an event to celebrate his 39th year as head of state. The length of Franco's rule far exceeded those of other, better-known, dictators: Hitler ruled Germany for 12 years, Mussolini was in power in Italy for 21 years and Stalin governed Russia for 24 years. There were seven main factors which explain the longevity of his regime.

Pragmatism

Franco was a cautious **pragmatist**. He tended to introduce policies which worked rather than policies that he believed in. His position in the Second World War is a good example. Franco was clearly sympathetic to Hitler and Mussolini. What is more, as a military leader, he was keen to take Spain into the war in order to restore her international glory. Nonetheless, as a pragmatist, Franco was only willing to enter the war on terms that would assure a good outcome for Spain. When Hitler refused to promise Franco the African territory that he wanted, Franco backed out of negotiations and Spain stayed neutral. As a result, Franco and the New State survived the war.

Economic policy is another good example of Franco's pragmatism. Franco believed strongly in autarky – Spain's economic self-reliance. Nonetheless, when it became clear that the policy was not working, he permitted reform. The new free-market policy was much less to Franco's liking, but he allowed it to continue because it ended the economic crisis of 1956 and resulted in an 'economic miracle' in the 1960s.

Political manipulation

The regime survived due to Franco's skilful political manipulation. Franco's regime was always made up of different factions. Franco used this to his advantage by playing them off against each other. In the early years of the regime, the monarchists posed the biggest threat to Franco's rule. Franco knew this and therefore he gave important jobs to the Falangists to balance the monarchists. Crucially, he put senior Falangists in charge of the media. As a result, the monarchists could not take their demands for an immediate restoration of the monarchy to the country.

However, when the Falangists overstepped the mark in the 1950s by publicly proposing the creation of a fully Falangist state, Franco sidelined the Falange and promoted the technocrats who were associated with Opus Dei. This enabled him to disassociate from fascism and win over the international community.

Franco's ability to play different factions off against each other helped him to survive because, by making and breaking alliances with the different factions, he was always able to control his government.

Repression

In its first years, Franco's regime survived due to ruthless repression. Franco's willingness to have hundreds of thousands of people executed for political crimes ensured that the opposition was completely crushed throughout the 1940s and early 1950s. During this period, socialists and anarchists were killed, imprisoned or too scared to oppose the regime. This policy was crucial in the early years because economic mismanagement led to poor harvests and mass hunger. The opposition organisations and leaders who could have capitalised on this discontent had been destroyed and as a result Franco survived.

Glossary

Pragmatism

The belief that the best course of action is the one that is the most likely to work. Pragmatism is often contrasted with idealism, that is the desire to do what is morally right regardless of the consequences.

Sir Samuel Hoare, British Ambassador in Madrid 1946, on the Franco regime

"If the strength of a government is the weakness of the opposition, the Franco regime was less precarious than many of its foreign critics and émigré opponents imagined."

Taking it further

In 1975, the Spanish population was surveyed:

Question:	Proportion agreeing:
Do you agree that Franco's death was a loss to Spain?	80%
Do you support the succession of Juan Carlos?	90%

These results appear to suggest a high level of popular support for Franco and for the succession that Franco initiated. How far are these statistics useful to a historian of Franco's Spain?

Propaganda

During the 1940s and 1950s government propaganda depicted Franco as Spain's saviour. Franco was the man who had saved Spain from communism, the man who had saved Spain from the destruction of the Second World War and the protector of traditional Spanish values. The Catholic Church was a great help in this depiction of Franco. The Church publicly supported Franco's crusade against communism, it allowed Franco to use religious imagery in his propaganda, and Church schools taught a conservative moral code which supported the government's social policy. In this sense, as mass terror subsided during the 1950s, the regime became more reliant on propaganda and the blessing of the Church as supports for its power.

Economic miracle

The economic miracle of the late 1950s also helped the regime survive. In truth, Franco had no interest in economics and had little responsibility for the economic miracle. At the same time, he was happy to take the credit for the boom. Therefore, in the 1960s, propaganda portrayed Franco as a wise leader who had created unprecedented prosperity, focusing much less on Franco as Spain's saviour.

The economic boom also helped the regime to survive because it created a 'feel-good factor'. Specifically, the vast majority of Spain's population were happy to put up with the dictatorship as long as they were growing richer.

Support of the elites

Franco's regime also survived because it had the support of powerful elites, at least for the better part of the regime.

- The support of the Catholic Church gave the regime a moral authority in the eyes of Spain's Catholic population.
- Franco's economic policy allowed big business to thrive and therefore won their backing.
- Franco had the support of the army. Franco continually spent a large proportion of the nation's budget on the military. Additionally, immediately after the civil war, he subordinated the Falange militia to the army – a measure which emphasised the army's importance and won the loyalty of the army hierarchy. On a personal level, senior army generals respected Franco because he had proved himself to be a skilled tactician and a capable leader during the civil war.

Weakness of the opposition

Finally, the opposition to Franco in the 1960s and 1970s was not strong enough to overthrow the regime.

- Student radicals were no match for the army and the police so, while they could embarrass the regime, they stood no chance of overthrowing it.
- Worker opposition forced small changes in pay and conditions, but they were not able to force significant political change.
- Radical priests put moral pressure on the regime, but in the short-term Franco could counter this with propaganda and the arrest of the priests.
- Even ETA, who successfully assassinated Carrero Blanco, could not force change on the regime. The assassination only prompted further repression.

The assassination of Carrero Blanco in December 1973

Conclusion: Why did Franco's death end the dictatorship?

By the early 1970s, the formula that had kept Franco in power for so long was breaking down. The Church deserted the regime in favour of democracy and, as the economy went into recession, the working class became increasingly dissatisfied. As a result, Franco's final years were some of the most difficult of his regime.

The government's plans to ensure a peaceful succession were undermined by the economic crisis, the steady decline in Franco's health, ETA's terrorist campaign and street fighting, the likes of which had not been seen since the civil war. The increasing opposition showed that the regime had lost the support of large sections of the population. What is more, international pressure meant that Franco could not use terror to control the population as he had in the 1940s.

Evidently, the regime, which had lasted almost 40 years, could not go on without reform. Juan Carlos knew this, and therefore the transition from dictatorship to monarchy was the beginning of the transition to democracy.

Activity: Franco – success or failure?

At the time of Franco's death in 1975, Spain was suffering from an economic recession, the government was divided, there was fighting on the streets, and the heavy-handed repression carried out by Arias Navarro's government had alienated foreign powers. Furthermore, Juan Carlos quickly started on the path to democracy, resulting, in the long-term, in the election of a left-wing government. In this sense, it is possible to view the Franco regime as a failure.

Look back over your notes from this course. Make a list of Franco's aims for Spain, and assess how far he had achieved these aims by 1975. How far do you agree with the view that Franco's government was a failure?

Activity: Franco's obituary

Imagine you are a journalist working in 1975. You have been asked to write an obituary for Franco. Produce a 500-word assessment of Franco's career since the outbreak of the Spanish Civil War. The obituary should be written from one of two perspectives:

- the perspective of the right-wing Spanish press – in this role, you will need to celebrate Franco's successes, and justify his policies of repression and economic control

- the perspective of the international press – in this role, you will need to produce a more objective account which recognises the successes and failures of the regime.

Activity: beginnings and endings

Imagine that you have been set the essay question: 'Why did Franco's regime last so long?' Your notes will form a plan for the main body of the essay.

Write an introduction and conclusion for the essay. Remember to explain which factor you think was most important.

Taking it further

Once you have completed this task, you could search online for actual obituaries of Franco from 1975, and compare them to the one you have written.

Skills Builder 4: **Extended writing**

So far, in the Skills Builders, you have learned about:

- the importance of writing in paragraphs
- answering questions on causation and change
- how to write introductions and conclusions.

Now you are going to learn about how to write a full response to an examination question. Remember you will only have 40 minutes for each answer so you need to make the most of your time.

Read the QUESTION PAPER thoroughly

You will have a choice of two questions on this topic, but you only need to answer one. Make sure that you make the right choice. Don't rush. Allow time – a few minutes – to decide which question to answer. You won't have time to change your mind halfway through the exam.

Read YOUR CHOSEN QUESTION thoroughly

Once you have made your choice, examine the question and work out what you are expected to do.

What is the question asking you to do?

There are a number of different types of question you could be asked. Examples are:

- How far?
- How important?
- How extensive?
- To what extent?
- Why?

Make sure that your answer is relevant to the type of question that has been asked.

In the first four question types, you will be expected to assess a range of factors. You will weigh up the importance of each factor you mention in relation to the question. You will need to reach a judgment on the question in hand. For instance:

> (A) 'Franco's regime lasted so long because he enjoyed the support of the Catholic Church.' How far do you agree with this opinion?

In answering this question, you will be expected to provide evidence of why the support of the Catholic Church was important in maintaining Franco's hold on power. You will also be expected to assess the extent to which other factors – for example, the 'economic miracle' from 1958, the use of terror and repression, and the weak and divided nature of opposition – played a role in the longevity of Franco's regime.

Make sure you cover the whole question

Here is an example:

> (B) How far do you agree that Franco modernised Spain in the period 1939–75?

In this question you must make sure that you explain both aspects of the question:

- ways in which Franco did modernise Spain
- evidence that Spain remained a country of traditional values.

Make a plan

Once you are clear about what the question is asking, sketch out what you intend to cover. Write down what you think will be relevant information in the form of a list or a concept map. Then organise your information in a way which best answers the question.

Writing the answer

Make sure that you include the following:

- Write a brief introduction, setting out your argument and what you will be discussing in your answer.
- Write a separate paragraph for each factor/reason you give. In the paragraph, make sure that you make a clear point and support it with specific examples.
- At the end of each paragraph, make a clear link between the point you have made and the question, showing how the point answers the question.
- Avoid just writing descriptions.
- Avoid merely 'telling a story'.
- Write a concluding paragraph which sums up your arguments and provides a clear judgment on the question.

Pace yourself

Success in an examination is based partly on effective time management. If you have approximately 40 minutes to answer a question, make sure that after about 12 or 13 minutes you have written about one-third of your answer. And after 35 minutes you should be thinking about and then writing your conclusion.

If you run short of time, make sure that you can still write a proper concluding paragraph. If necessary, you can save time by cutting short your treatment of the paragraph or paragraphs before, by:

- writing the first sentence containing your point
- bullet-pointing your evidence for this point – the information that backs it up
- writing the last sentence of the paragraph which explains the link between your point and the question.

EXAM SUCCESS!

- Timing: pace yourself.
- Be clear about the focus of the question you have chosen.
- Make a brief plan of your answer before starting to write.

Activity: Write your own introduction

Write an introduction to the following question:

> (A) How successful was the Franco regime in assuring a peaceful transition to monarchy in the years 1969–75?

You will need to draw on your knowledge of the nature and course of the war, and the factors leading to Nationalist victory. You will need to summarise evidence for and against the argument stated in the question.

Activity: Write your own conclusion

Write a conclusion of not more than four sentences to the following question. Try to write it in five minutes.

> (B) How accurate is it to say that Spain experienced an 'economic miracle' in the years 1956–75?

Activity: Write an introduction and conclusion

Here is another example of a question:

> (C) How extensive was repression in Franco's Spain in the period 1939–57?

Now write an introduction and a conclusion – each in approximately five minutes.

Tip – plan the conclusion first. You will always find it easier to write an introduction once you have decided what your conclusion will be. This is because, once you know where your answer is going, you can introduce it.

Activity: Write your own answer

Now write your own answer to this question, following the guidance given above:

> (D) How far did Franco's government relax government controls in the period 1957–75?

Examzone

Now that you have finished the course content, you will have to do the last bits of preparation for the exam itself. This advice covers two important elements for exam success: revising the information and using your information well in the examination.

This topic – 'Republicanism, Civil War and Francoism in Spain, 1931–75' – is part of Edexcel's Option E/F: The Expansion and Challenge of Nationalism, in Unit 1. The Unit 1 exam will be 1 hour and 20 minutes in length, and is worth 60 marks in total.

In the exam you will be given the choice of two questions on the topic 'Republicanism, Civil War and Francoism in Spain'. You will be expected to answer one of these and should spend no more than half the examination time answering it. You will also have to answer another question from a different topic. You will be expected to answer the questions you choose in essay form.

What to expect

You will need to remember information, but the exam is mainly testing whether or not you can apply the relevant information in answering a question. You will be assessed on your ability to recall and select historical knowledge and to deploy it (i.e. make use of knowledge to support your points). You can see that it's not just knowing what happened which counts, but understanding how to use what you know.

You will also be assessed on your ability to present historical explanations that show an understanding of history. You should read the question carefully to make sure you answer it in the right way. Sometimes questions will simply begin 'Why'. These are asking you to analyse the causes of an event or development. For the highest marks you will need to show how factors combined to bring about the event.

Most questions will ask you for a judgment. Here are some different types of question stem you may come across in the exam:

1. How far was x responsible for y?
2. To what extent did x change?
3. How far did x depend on y?
4. Did x play a major part in y?

Although judgment questions come in a variety of forms, they are all asking you to balance points. In the case of example 2 below, you will be looking for evidence of change and of continuity in order to reach a judgment about the extent of change.

When you choose your question in the examination, take note of what sort of judgment it asks you to make. The essay questions test a variety of skills. Here are some examples of different skills being tested by the questions.

1. The analysis of, and judgment about, the **key features** of a situation.
   For example: *To what extent is it accurate to describe the Franco regime in the period 1939–75 as 'totalitarian'?*
2. The analysis of, and judgment about, the **extent of change**.
   For example: *How far do you agree that Franco improved the Spanish economy in the period 1939–75?*
3. The analysis of **consequences or effects**.
   For example: *How accurate is it to say that foreign intervention was the key factor determining the outcome of the Spanish Civil War?*
4. The analysis of, and judgment about, the causes of a historical event or situation.
   For example: *How far were mistakes made by Republicans responsible for the weakness of the Second Republic in the period 1931–36?*

Another type of question will ask you how far you agree with a statement. This is still a judgment question. You should clarify what the statement is about so that you know what the question expects of you:

- Is it a statement about causation, like this question: *How far do you agree that the growing fear of communism in Spain explains the fall of the Second Republic?*
- Or is it about change like this question: *How far do you agree that the Second Republic failed to transform Spain in the period 1931–36?*

When you are clear about what the question wants from you, you can use what you have learned in the Skills Builder sections of this book to produce an answer based on extended writing (an essay) which will help you to gain high marks.

How to revise

Make a revision plan

Before you start revising, make a plan. Otherwise it is easy to waste your precious revision time. It is helpful to look at your exam dates and work backwards to the first date you intend to start revising. Here are some tips on how to create a revision plan:

1. First, fill in the dates of your examinations and then any regular commitments you have. This will help give you a realistic idea of how much time you have to revise.

2. Plan your time carefully, assigning more time to topics you find difficult.

3. Use a revision 'checklist'. Look at what you need to know and try to identify any gaps in your knowledge.

4. Now fill in the timetable with sensible work slots and breaks.

5. Keep to this timetable! Organise yourself well and it will help you to fulfil your potential. If you have not prepared a revision plan yet, it is not too late to start. Put your plan up somewhere visible so you can refer back to it.

Revision tips

- Revise often – try to do a little every day.

- Make sure you have one day a week when you don't do revision or even think about exams – you'll come back to it refreshed.

- Take a 5- or 10-minute break every hour, and do some stretching exercises, go for a short walk or make a drink.

- Talk to your family or a friend about your revision – they may be able to help you. For example, they could test you on key facts.

- Keep bullet points on 'crib cards' highlighting important revision points. For example, you could have a list or a concept map of the reasons why the Nationalists won the civil war. Use these for quick revision and for reading during 'dead' times – when you're waiting for a bus, for example.

- Use mnemonics. This is when you take the first letter of a series of words you want to remember and then make a new sentence. A common mnemonic for remembering the order of the points of the compass (North, East, South, and West) is 'Naughty Elephants Squirt Water'. You could use a mnemonic to help you remember the reasons for the outbreak of the civil war.

- Some people revise well by listening, so you could try 'talking' your revision and recording it onto an mp3 player if you have one. Listen to these while lying in bed, while travelling in a car or walking to the shops. This also takes the guilt out of being out and about rather than in front of your books!

- Practise your exam techniques. As you revise key topics, plan five or six points to make about the causes / consequences / key features / changes relating to major developments. You could use question stems 1–4 on the previous page, and slot in your own x and y.

- Try doing some timed essays. This will make it easier to write a good essay when it comes to the exam.

- Don't panic. Think about what you can achieve, not what you can't. Positive thinking is important! Remember, the examiner will be looking to reward you for what you can do.

Assessment objectives

To do well in your exam, you need to make sure you meet all the assessment objectives. Below are the assessment objectives you need to meet and some advice on how to make sure you meet them.

Recall, select and deploy historical knowledge
AO1a

In your essay, you must show that you can remember, choose and use historical knowledge.

- Remember – *recollect historical facts from your study of this unit*
- Choose – *select specific facts that are relevant to the essay you are writing*
- Use – *place these facts in your essay in a way that supports your argument*

Understanding of the past
AO1b (i)

You need to show that you understand the period studied. Simply telling the story of what happened will not help you to do this. Instead, you need to:

- Analyse – *break down the topic you are considering into key points*
- Explain – *suggest reasons why these key points provide an answer to the question*
- Reach a judgment – *decide which of your key points was most important and provide reasons to support this*

As you think about analysis, explanation and judgment, remember to bear in mind the relevant **key concepts** and **relationships**.

Key concepts
AO1b (ii)

When faced with an essay question, consider which of the following key concepts it focuses on:

- Causation – *what made an event happen?*
- Consequence – *what were the results of this event?*
- Continuity – *in what ways did things stay the same?*
- Change – *in what ways were things different?*
- Significance – *why was this important?*

Then ensure that your answer remains focused on this concept.

Relationships
AO1b (iii)

Once you have planned the key points you will make in your essay, consider the following:

- How do these key points link together?
- Which key point was most important? Why?

Once you have considered these issues, arrange your points in an order that reflects the way they link together or the relative importance of each key point.

Level descriptors

Each essay you write in the exam will be given a mark out of 30 and will correspond to a level from 1 to 5, with level 5 being the highest. Here is some information about what the levels mean. Read it carefully and use this information to aim for the top!

Level 1:
) General points about the historical period that are correct but not necessarily focused on the topic raised by the question.
) The general points will not be supported by accurate and relevant specific examples.

Answers at this level will be very simplistic, irrelevant or vague.

Level 2:
) A number of general points about the topic of the question.
) The general points will be supported by some accurate and relevant examples.

Answers at this level might tell the story or part of the story without addressing the question, or might list the key points without backing them up with specific examples.

Level 3:
) A number of points with some focus on the question.
) The points will be supported by accurate material, but some whole paragraphs may be either only partly relevant, lacking in detail or both.

At Level 3 answers will attempt to focus on the question and have some strengths (some paragraphs will have point, supporting evidence and linkage back to the question), but answers will also have significant areas of weakness. For example, the focus on the question may drift, the answer may lack specific examples or parts of the essay may simply tell the story.

Level 4:
) A number of points which clearly address the question and show an understanding of the most important factors involved.
) The points will be supported by accurate material which will be mostly relevant and detailed.
) There will be clear explanation of how the points and specific examples provide an answer to the question.

At Level 4 answers will clearly attempt to tackle the question and demonstrate a detailed knowledge of the period studied.

Level 5:
) A number of points which clearly address the question and show a thorough understanding of the most important factors involved.
) The points will be supported by accurate material which will be relevant and detailed.
) There will be clear explanation of how the points and specific examples provide an answer to the question, as well as an evaluation of the relative importance of the different factors or issues discussed.

Answers that are judged to be Level 5 will be thorough and detailed – they will clearly engage with the specific question, providing a balanced and carefully reasoned argument that reaches a clear and supported judgment.

Sample answer 1

How far do you agree that Franco's Spain was totalitarian?

An answer given a mark in Level 5 of the published mark scheme

Franco's Spain was never fully totalitarian. A totalitarian state is a regime in which the government has complete control over all aspects of life, including the economy, society and politics. Between 1939 and 1945, the government enjoyed a considerable degree of control in these areas. However, from the late 1950s onwards, Franco allowed a large degree of liberalisation in most areas of Spanish life. Even in the first years after the civil war, the independence enjoyed by the Church and big business indicates that Spain under Franco cannot be described as a totalitarian state.

EXAMINER COMMENT

This introduction is clearly focused on the question. It offers a definition of totalitarianism, and an overview of the period specified in the question, as well as a preliminary judgment concerning the extent to which Spain under Franco can be called totalitarian.

Franco's government had enormous control over Spanish society through repression, particularly in the years immediately following the civil war. The Law of Political Responsibilities (February 1939) gave the government the power to persecute people who had formerly supported the Republic. Between 1939 and 1945, around 500,000 people were convicted of breaking this law, and over 200,000 were executed. This period came to be known as 'a time of silence' because the extensive repression crushed all opposition to the regime. This period saw Spain at its most totalitarian due to the high levels of government control enforced through terror. However, after 1945, terror declined and therefore in the later part of the period, political opposition reappeared in Spain. During the 1960's, the number of hours lost due to strike action increased from approximately 2.5 million in 1967 to almost 7 million in 1970. What is more, the terrorist organisation ETA was able to attract more than 2,000 members by 1970, with only limited opposition from Franco's police. Evidently, the extent of repression declined as the regime progressed and, therefore, following 1945, it would be wrong to describe Spain as totalitarian.

EXAMINER COMMENT

Precisely selected information supports the student's claims about the extent of government control exerted through repression and terror. The argument is sophisticated because it recognises that the nature of Franco's regime changed over time although the inclusion of strike action is not made directly relevant to political opposition.

In the economy, too, there was an early totalitarian period, followed by later liberalisation. In 1939, Franco and the Falange introduced autarky and corporatism. These two economic policies were favoured by the Falange, who wanted to establish a totalitarian state, including complete control over the economy. Autarky, which means economic self-sufficiency, gave the government complete control over imports and exports, while corporatism destroyed independent trades unions, giving the government greater control over the workers. However, following the economic crisis of 1957, Opus Dei technocrats liberalised the Spanish economy, introducing a free market. They encouraged Spanish businesses to trade with the West, ending autarky, and reduced government control of the domestic economy, significantly weakening corporatism. In this way, the totalitarianism of early economic policy gave way to free market capitalism and therefore, following 1957, the Spanish economy cannot be described as totalitarian.

Franco's policy of 'purging' Spanish society between 1939 and 1945 also gave the government considerable control over Spanish society. For example, the government significantly reduced the freedom of women. By reintroducing the 1889 Civil Code, women became legally dependent on their fathers and then their husbands. In addition, a reintroduction of the 1870 Criminal Code made adultery a criminal offence and homosexuality was outlawed from 1954. However, following the government's emphasis on tourism in the late 1950s, social policy in Spain liberalised. For example, it became more acceptable for women to wear bikinis in coastal resorts. Also, although pornography and contraception were still technically illegal, the government did little to police their availability. Again, Franco's early attempts to enforce strict control over the Spanish people gave way to a more liberal approach, and therefore Spanish society was not fully totalitarian.

EXAMINER COMMENT

In the above paragraphs, the candidate once again considers evidence for and against the statement that Spain was totalitarian, as well as supporting the arguments with specific information and accurate terminology.

The Church enjoyed a considerable degree of political independence throughout the Franco regime. In 1953, Franco signed a concordat, which guaranteed that the government would not interfere with the Catholic Church. A decade later, radical priests used the freedom given to the Church to criticise the regime. The independence of the Church, which pre-dated the concordat, showed that in an important area of life, the government never enjoyed total control, and therefore that the Franco regime was never fully totalitarian.

In politics too, there was considerable liberalisation as the period progressed. During the Spanish Civil War, Franco created a national movement which united the various Nationalist factions and became the only accept political organisation during Franco's rule. Nonetheless, there was a great deal of diversity within the movement, and some freedom of debate between monarchists, Falangists, Carlists and - later - Opus Dei technocrats. During the 1960s, attempts were made to officially liberalise Spanish politics. The 1964 Law of Associations legalised the formation of small groups, which later became the basis for independent political parties. Equally, the 1966 Press Act ended a great deal of censorship, allowing considerable freedom of discussion. The political uniformity required for totalitarianism was never fully achieved in Franco's Spain.

EXAMINER COMMENT

These two paragraphs provide a balance in the treatment of the years 1939–45. Earlier paragraphs suggest that this was the totalitarian period. However, by considering the Church and politics, the candidate shows an awareness that this interpretation is too simplistic.

In conclusion, between 1939 and 1945, the Franco government enjoyed a considerable amount of control over the society and the economy, partly due to the high levels of repression that it employed. However, even in this early period, there was some freedom of political discussion within the National Movement, and the Church enjoyed considerable independence. Therefore, even in this early period, the Franco regime cannot be described as totalitarian. The later period saw considerable economic and social liberalisation, as well as political reform. Consequently, it is inaccurate to describe Franco's Spain as totalitarian in the period 1939-75.

EXAMINER COMMENT

This response was awarded a mark in Level 5 of the mark scheme [25–30 marks]. It is continually focused on the question, and uses the definition of totalitarianism set out in the introduction to reach a fully supported judgment about the extent to which Franco's Spain was totalitarian. The response shows range and depth of knowledge, and deals with the whole period from 1939 to 1975.

Sample answer 2

How far do you agree that Franco's Spain was totalitarian?

An answer given a mark in Level 3 of the published mark scheme

Franco came to power in Spain in 1939 after three years of bitter civil war. Historians are divided over whether Franco's Spain was totalitarian or not. He certainly received aid from Germany and Italy who were totalitarian powers. But the introduction of bikinis in the 1960s suggests that he was more liberal. In this essay, I will discuss how far Franco's Spain was totalitarian and how far it wasn't.

EXAMINER COMMENT

This is not a good introduction. Rather than answering the question, the candidate provides two specific pieces of information – one from outside the period, the other slightly inaccurate – and then states the purpose of the essay rather than the judgment it will reach.

During the civil war, and in the years after the civil war, women were oppressed by Franco's nationalist regime. Whereas, in the Second Republic and in the Republican zone during the war, women could wear trousers and smoke cigarettes, under Franco, women were made legally inferior to men. They were not allowed to have abortions or to divorce their husbands, or even to have affairs. However, the number of women attending universities in the 1960s did increase, and by 1970, around a third of university students were female. In this way, there were some opportunities for women in Franco's Spain.

Tourism also brought about change in Spain. As people came to Spain from Western Europe, countries like France, Britain and Germany, they brought with them new ideas which were more liberal. Bikinis were worn by foreigners on beaches. Priests were shocked and said that women were becoming 'carnal goddesses'. Tourism also turned Spain into a land of sand, sun and sex, and package holidays. This is not what Franco had envisaged during his Catholic crusade in the Spanish Civil War, when he wanted to give the Church more of a say over Spanish morality.

EXAMINER COMMENT

In both of these paragraphs, the student has introduced some relevant information, and has provided some detailed examples. However, the paragraphs lack clear focus on the question.

Some aspects of Franco's economy were totalitarian. In the early years, Franco adopted some policies to try to improve Spain's economy – corporatism and autarky. These policies gave the government a lot of power over the economy, and therefore can be considered totalitarian. However, after an economic crisis, things changed as the free market began to operate, and the government had a lot less control over the economy, and therefore the economy was no longer totalitarian.

EXAMINER COMMENT

This paragraph focuses on the question and implicitly defines totalitarianism. However, it provides little specific information to support its points.

One part of the regime which was always totalitarian was Franco's use of repression. Throughout this period, Franco used laws to persecute his political opponents. After 1939, 500,000 people were arrested for political crimes, and 200,000 were executed. Franco even turned against the Church, sending priests to the so-called Concordat Jail. In 1974, he used the garrotte vil to execute Salvador Puig Antich, an anarchist who had killed a policeman. Franco's continuous use of repression was the most totalitarian part of his government.

EXAMINER COMMENT

This paragraph also focuses well on the question. However, it is extremely one-sided, and therefore inaccurate in its conclusion.

Overall, I feel that Franco's regime was totalitarian because of the continuous repression, although women and the economy were not so totalitarian and the Church enjoyed a lot of freedom except for those priests sent to the Concordat Jail.

EXAMINER COMMENT

This response was awarded a mark in Level 3 of the mark scheme [13–18 marks]. The candidate clearly has some understanding of the requirements of the question. However, none of the paragraphs meet all of these requirements. In the earlier paragraphs, the candidate displays detailed knowledge without a precise focus on the question. In the later paragraphs, the focus improves, but the level of detail drops or becomes extremely one-sided. Due to the fact that the essay covers a good range of relevant factors, and that there is some detail and some focus, it meets the criteria for high Level 3 and was given 17 marks.

Index

industrialists 7, 10, 22
industry 6, 14, 19, 24, 37, 47, 60, 76, 83, 85–6
inflation 82, 95
International Brigades 46, 53, 55, 57–8
International Symposium 91
investment 6, 76, 82–5, 87, 95
Italy 22, 25–6, 37, 53–6, 71, 73, 77, 96

La Niña Bonita 12
Labour Day 38
labourers 6, 12, 14–15, 19, 23, 37, 81, 83
landowners 7–8, 10, 13, 15–18, 20, 22–3, 37–8, 64, 66–7, 79
Largo Caballero, Francisco 13, 15–16, 23, 25–6, 31, 38, 43, 49, 51, 57, 63
Law of Associations 81, 87
Law of Leadership Succession 72–3, 92–3
Law of Municipal Boundaries 21, 23
Law of Political Responsibilities 72, 76, 80
Law, Oliver 55–6
Lerroux, Alejandro 13, 22–3, 26
Los Años de Hambre 76

Madrid, fall of 50
marriage 8, 19, 65, 74, 78–9, 87
Marshall Plan 72, 78
martial law 64, 89
Marxists 31, 42–3, 74
May Day 38
middle class 6, 8, 13, 36–8, 40, 44
military coup 5, 7, 30, 34, 64
modernisation 6, 85–6
Mola, General Emilio 30, 32–4, 40–1, 45–7, 51, 55–6
monarchists 16, 32, 36, 44, 51, 73–4, 77, 97
monarchy 4–5, 7–15, 17, 20–2, 32, 37, 72–4, 77, 92–3, 97, 99
Montseny, Federica 63
Morocco 8–9, 18, 34–7, 40–1, 77
Movimiento Nacional 44
Mujeres Libres 63
Mussolini, Benito 26, 37, 39, 53–4, 56, 96–7

national identity 6
National Movement 81–2, 88–9
nationalism 5, 10, 17, 24, 32, 39, 67, 88–90
Negrín Lopez, Juan 49–51, 57
neutrality 77
New State 3, 73–4, 76, 78–80, 82, 97
Nin, Andreu 43
Non-Intervention Pact 53–5, 57

Ochoa, General Lopez 24
Opus Dei 81–2, 94, 97
Organic Law 81, 88
Orwell, George 57–8, 61–2

Pamplona 32, 34–6, 40–1, 45, 47, 59, 67
parliament 7, 14, 17, 88
peasants 8–9, 13, 15–16, 18–19, 23, 27, 31, 36–8, 40, 61, 63–4, 67, 76
persecution 50, 74, 79
political manipulation 72, 97
political terror 66
Popular Army 49–51, 62–3
Popular Front 21, 25–6, 30–1, 33, 53
POUM 43, 57, 59, 62–3, 69
poverty 5–6, 31, 62, 85, 90
Press Law 72, 74
propaganda 19, 22, 32, 42, 64, 66–8, 72–4, 79–80, 90, 96–8
prosperity 6, 83–4, 98
prostitution 63, 65
Provisional Government 12–13, 15
PSOE 13, 15, 43, 49, 69
public services 60
Puig Antich, Salvador 92, 95
purification 76

racism 55
Radical Republican Party 13, 22–3, 26
reactionary right 21
rebellion 21, 24, 27, 32–4, 36, 41, 55–6, 64
recession 24, 95, 99
Red Terror 66–7
reformers 13, 20, 38, 93
Religious Freedom Act 81, 88
repression 3, 17, 63, 72, 89, 95–9
Republican Action Party 13, 22
republicanism 4, 13, 102
revolution 15, 17, 31, 38, 42–4, 59–63, 66, 68
Ruiz, Solis 89
ruling elites 7, 9
Russia 31, 38, 53–8, 71, 77, 96

San Sebastian 13, 23, 35, 59
sanitation 6, 85
Sanjurjo, General José 12, 18, 32, 44
Saragossa 14–15, 48–9
Segura, Cardinal 16
separation of powers 88
separatists 10, 17
shanty town 84

social policy 7, 78–9, 87, 98
socialism 31, 37, 59
Socialist Party 13, 23–4
society 3, 8, 11–12, 14, 24, 27, 29, 33, 36, 38–40, 60–2, 67, 69, 74, 76–7, 79, 81, 85–6, 88
Spanish army 9, 18, 34
Spanish Communist Party 43, 49, 63
Sperrle, Hugo 46–8, 51
Stabilisation Plan 81, 83
Stalin, Josef 38, 54, 96
Strait of Gibraltar 35–6, 37, 47–8, 59
Student Union 89
students 3, 65, 70, 85, 88–90
Suarez, Adolfo 93
succession 32, 92–5, 99
Syndical Organisation 64, 89

technocrats 82–4, 97
terror 3, 59, 66–8, 73–4, 76, 91, 98–9
totalitarianism 75, 80
tourism 83–7, 95
trade 6, 9, 17, 37, 43, 60, 63–4, 66, 68, 75–6, 82–3, 86
trade unions 9, 24–5
Tragic Week 9
transport 37, 60
Treaty of Madrid 78
Trotsky, Leon 43, 54
Trotskyites 57, 71

UGT 9, 15, 17, 24, 32
unemployment 6, 10, 14, 38, 84
United Nations 72, 78
United States 9, 55

war of attrition 46, 48
welfare 85
White Terror 66–8
women's rights 87
working class 6, 19, 31, 37, 43, 61, 68, 75

Published by Pearson Education Limited, a company incorporated in England and Wales, having its registered office at Edinburgh Gate, Harlow, Essex, CM20 2JE. Registered company number: 872828

www.pearsonschoolsandfecolleges.co.uk

Edexcel is a registered trademark of Edexcel Limited

Text © Pearson Education Limited 2011

First published 2011

13 12 11

10 9 8 7 6 5 4 3 2 1

British Library Cataloguing in Publication Data
A catalogue record for this book is available from the British Library

ISBN 978 1 84690 751 7

Edited by Polly Hennessy
Typeset by Ian Foulis
Original illustrations © Pearson Education 2010
Illustrated by Ian Foulis
Printed and bound at Henry Ling, Dorset, UK

Acknowledgements
The author and publisher would like to thank the following individuals and organisations for permission to reproduce photographs:

akg-images Ltd: 7, 25; **Bridgeman Art Library Ltd**: 15; **Bundesarchiv (Federal Archives)**: Bild 183-C0214-0007-013 54, Bild 183-C02426 44, Bild 183-R98690 77; **Corbis**: Bettmann 18, 31, 35, 47, 68, Hulton-Deutsch Collection 74, JUAN GUZMAN / EFE 60; **Agencia EFE**: 19, 24; **Mary Evans Picture Library**: © Thomas Cook Archive / Illustrated London News Ltd 86; **Getty Images**: Hulton Archive 72, 98, Gamma-Keystone 22, 92, 96; **TopFoto**: 23, © 2004 TopFoto 73; UCL Library Services: 61; **New York University, The Tamiment Library & Robert F. Wagner Labor Archives**: Paul Burns Photographs Collection, Abraham Lincoln Brigade Archives, Tamiment Library, New York University 55

Cover images: Front: **Getty Images**: W. Eugene Smith

All other images © Pearson Education

The author and publisher would like to thank the following individuals and organisations for permission to reproduce copyrighted material:

Figures
Maps in unit 6 from *The Spanish Civil War*, Third Edition 1977, Penguin Books 1965 (Thomas, H.) pp.833, 885, copyright © Hugh Thomas, 1961, 1965, 1977. Reproduced by permission of Penguin Group (UK) Ltd.

Tables
Table in unit 10 from *The Franco Regime 1936–1975*, University of Wisconsin Press (Payne, S.G.) pp.485-486, copyright © 1987 by the Board of Regents of the University of Wisconsin System. Reproduced by permission of The University of Wisconsin Press.

Text
Extracts in units 7, 8 from *Homage to Catalonia* (George Orwell) copyright © George Orwell, 1937, by permission of Bill Hamilton as the Literary Executor of the Estate of the Late Sonia Brownell Orwell and Secker & Warburg Ltd; and copyright © 1952 and renewed 1980 by Sonia Brownell Orwell, reprinted by permission of Houghton Mifflin Harcourt Publishing Company.

Every effort has been made to contact copyright holders of material reproduced in this book. Any omissions will be rectified in subsequent printings if notice is given to the publishers.